WALKS *for* EACH SEASON

26 great days out in
the countryside near London

Second Edition

JULIA SMITH

This book is dedicated

To my parents, Ruth and Brian Smith, who took us (me, my brother and my sister) walking in the countryside from an early age, showing us how to enjoy it, to feel as though it was ours in some way, and instilling a healthy sense of entitlement to roam – what gifts.

Harlington
24
BEDS
Tring
3
HERTS
ESSEX
19
Wendover
BUCKS
2
Chorleywood
Cookham
23
LONDON
Benfleet
18
Richmond
16
BERKS
Cuxton
10
Shoreham
13
9
Otford
SURREY
25
Coulsdon
17
15
East Farleigh
20
26
Sevenoaks
Guildford
Box Hill
5
Penshurst
KENT
1
Eridge
W.SUSSEX
Lewes
E.SUSSEX
Winchelsea
8
14
22
Falmer

7
Manningtree
12
Frinton-
on-Sea
Faversham
21
4
Chartham
6
Deal
Folkestone
11

THE WALKS

TABLE OF WALKS

	WALK	PAGE	SEASONAL FEATURE	NAME	COUNTY	TRAVEL FROM
SPRING	1	16	Early spring flowers	Eridge Circular	East Sussex	London Bridge
	2	20	Celandines	Chorleywood to Little Chalfont	Herts & Bucks	Metropolitan line or Marylebone
	3	24	Bluebells	Tring Circular	Herts & Bucks	Euston
	4	30	Apple blossom	Chartham to Canterbury	Kent	St Pancras or Charing Cross
	5	36	Cow parsley	Penshurst to Leigh	Kent	London Bridge
	6	40	Seaside & chalkland flowers	Deal to Dover	Kent	St Pancras
SUMMER	7	48	Damselflies & dragonflies	Manningtree Circular	Essex & Suffolk	Liverpool Street
	8	54	Seaside & cliff walk	Winchelsea to Hastings	East Sussex	St Pancras
	9	58	Summer meadows	Otford Circular	Kent	Victoria
	10	62	Poppies & wildflower meadows	Cuxton Circular	Kent	St Pancras
	11	68	Seaside, art & fossils	Folkestone Circular	Kent	St Pancras or Charing Cross
	12	74	Seaside & fossils	Frinton-on-Sea to Walton-on-the-Naze	Essex	Liverpool Street
	13	82	Lavender fields	Shoreham to Eynsford	Kent	Blackfriars, Victoria or London Bridge
	14	85	Chalkland flowers	Lewes Circular	East Sussex	Victoria
AUTUMN	15	92	Apple orchards	East Farleigh to Yalding	Kent	Charing Cross or St Pancras
	16	98	Deer rut	Richmond Circular	London	District Line, London Overground or Waterloo
	17	104	Sweet chestnuts & deer rut	Sevenoaks Circular	Kent	Charing Cross
	18	108	Brent geese	Benfleet to Southend	Essex	Fenchurch Street
	19	114	Autumn leaves	Wendover to Princes Risborough	Bucks	Marylebone
	20	120	Autumn leaves	Guildford to Chilworth	Surrey	Waterloo
WINTER	21	126	Migrant waders & ducks	Faversham Circular	Kent	St Pancras or Victoria
	22	130	Starling murmuration	Falmer to Brighton	East Sussex	Victoria, Thameslink or London Bridge
	23	136	Thameside walk	Cookham Circular	Berkshire	Paddington
	24	139	For snow or frost	Harlington Circular	Beds	Thameslink
	25	143	For snow or frost	Coulsdon Circular	London	Thameslink. Victoria or London Bridge
	26	147	Catkins & winter trees	Box Hill Circular	Surrey	Victoria or Waterloo

TERRAIN	MILES	DIFFICULTY
Mainly level with some gentle ascents, quiet lanes, meadows, wild patches and woods in the High Weald	6	Easy
Mostly level but with two hills, meadows, woods, Chenies village and suburban streets	6½	Moderate
Some steep climbs, chalk downland, pasture and Chiltern beechwoods	10½ or 9	Moderate
Mainly level, riverside walk, orchards, roads, North Downs woodland and Canterbury's Riverside Gardens, several stiles	5 or 8	Easy
Initially flat then a number of short climbs up and down the undulating High Weald. Lots of stiles	8½	Moderate
Level seafront then gently undulating along the White Cliffs of Dover. A few short climbs and steep stairs down to St Margaret's Bay, ends with Dover streets	6 or 11	Easy/ Moderate
Mainly level, one gentle climb, riverside walk, Dedham village, paddocks and woodland	8	Easy
Initially fairly level. Steep ups and downs on the clifftop, town and village streets, grazing marsh, pebble beach and wooded gills	12	Strenuous
Steep ascents and undulating downland with meadows, pasture and woods in the North Downs	5½ or 7½	Moderate
Several climbs, most gradual, over the North Downs, across meadows, fields and through woodland	6	Moderate
Mainly level, one steep climb, Folkestone streets and seafront, wilder beach with some small boulders, concrete sea defences, a wood and clifftop walking	9½	Moderate
A level walk, but three flights of stairs, beside the sea along the promenade, then on pavements, wilder beach, salt marsh and coastal heath	6 or 7½	Easy
Level, one climb that can be avoided, riverside walking, farmland and pavements	5	Easy
Long climbs up to the South Downs, downland, farmland, pavements, quiet roads	4 or 8½ or 15½	Moderate/ Strenuous
Undulating, country roads, meadows, Loose village, orchards and woods along the Greensand Ridge	12	Easy
Mainly flat, gentle climb up to Richmond Park, parkland, woodland garden, Richmond streets and Thameside walk	8	Easy
Mainly level, Sevenoaks main street, Knole Park parkland and wooded Greensand Ridge	6 or 8½ or 10½	Easy
Level, but with one climb up to Hadleigh Castle and another up through Southend's cliff garden, salt marsh, fields and seaside promenade	5½ or 7½	Easy
Fairly level with one steep and one long gentle climb. Chiltern's downland escarpment and beechwoods	8½	Moderate
Fairly level with a couple of climbs. Surrey Hills escarpment, woods, lakes and a little riverside walking	6	Moderate
Mainly level, along Faversham streets and across fields, flat creekside and estuary walk through salt marsh and grazing marsh	6½ or 8	Easy
Mainly level but with a couple of climbs up the South Downs, downland, fields and seaside resort	6	Moderate
Mainly level, with one avoidable climb up an escarpment. Cookham streets, downland, grazing marsh and Thameside walk	5½	Easy
Several slow climbs, fields, downland escarpment and woods	5½ or 8	Moderate
A few moderate ups and downs on this otherwise fairly flatish walk. Downland, farmland and woods	5½ or 6½	Easy/Moderate
Steep hills in wooded North Downs, water meadow, heath and downland	9	Strenuous

CALENDAR OF WALKS

<table>
<tr><th>SEASON</th><th>MONTH</th><th>WEEK</th><th colspan="4">WALKS</th></tr>
<tr><td rowspan="9">SPRING</td><td>March</td><td>4</td><td rowspan="2">Walk 1
Early spring flowers</td><td></td><td></td><td></td></tr>
<tr><td rowspan="4">April</td><td>1</td><td rowspan="2">Walk 2
Celandines</td><td></td><td></td></tr>
<tr><td>2</td><td></td><td></td><td></td></tr>
<tr><td>3</td><td></td><td></td><td></td><td></td></tr>
<tr><td>4</td><td>Walk 3
Bluebells</td><td>Walk 4
Apple blossom</td><td></td><td></td></tr>
<tr><td rowspan="4">May</td><td>1</td><td></td><td></td><td></td><td></td></tr>
<tr><td>2</td><td rowspan="3">Walk 5
Cow parsley & hawthorn</td><td></td><td></td><td></td></tr>
<tr><td>3</td><td></td><td></td><td></td></tr>
<tr><td>4</td><td>Walk 6
Seaside flowers</td><td></td><td></td></tr>
<tr><td rowspan="9">SUMMER</td><td rowspan="4">June</td><td>1</td><td rowspan="3">Walk 7
Damselflies & dragonflies</td><td rowspan="2">Walk 8
Seaside & cliff walk</td><td></td><td rowspan="9">Walks 11 & 12
Seaside, art & fossils</td></tr>
<tr><td>2</td><td></td></tr>
<tr><td>3</td><td rowspan="3">Walk 9
Summer meadows</td><td rowspan="4">Walk 10
Poppies (weeks 3/4) & wildflower meadows</td></tr>
<tr><td>4</td><td></td></tr>
<tr><td rowspan="4">July</td><td>1</td><td rowspan="2">Walk 13
Lavender fields</td></tr>
<tr><td>2</td><td></td></tr>
<tr><td>3</td><td></td><td></td><td></td></tr>
<tr><td>4</td><td></td><td></td><td></td></tr>
<tr><td>Aug</td><td>Any week</td><td>Walk 14
Chalkland flowers</td><td></td><td></td></tr>
</table>

SEASON	MONTH	WEEK	WALKS			
AUTUMN	Sept	1	**Walk 15** Apple orchards			
		2				
		3				
		4				
	Oct	1	**Walk 16** Deer rut			
		2				
		3		**Walk 17** Sweet chestnuts & deer rut	**Walk 18** Brent geese	
		4				**Walks 19 & 20** Autumn leaves
	Nov	1				
		2-4				
WINTER	Dec	Any week	**Walk 21** Migrant waders & ducks	**Walk 22** Starling murmura-tion	**Walk 23** Thameside walk **Walks 24 & 25** For snow or frost	
	Jan	2				
		3				
		4				**Walk 26** Catkins & winter trees
	Feb	1				
		2				
		3				
		4				
	March	1-3				

INTRODUCTION

Seasons in the city are tamed and reduced and their signs are easy to miss. So when I ventured out from London to seek bluebells, orchards in blossom or to forage for sweet chestnuts, I often got it wrong.

I arrived too late or too early, or else I chose the wrong walk. My mistakes were the impetus for this book – so never again would I miss these seasonal classics or less celebrated marvels.

After walking more than a thousand miles over several springs, summers, autumns and winters, I've selected 26 beautiful walks that showcase the best of each season. I hadn't grasped just how transitory many seasonal events are. Peak autumn colour only lasts a fortnight and by the end of September orchards no longer burst with fruit, so I've also tried to work out the optimum time to appreciate each spectacle.

To avoid adding to London's pollution, all the walks start and end at a train station. This way you also bypass the traffic hell of driving back into the city. Rail fares can be cut by a third with one of the railcards on offer.

During this quest it dawned on me that London is the ideal base from which to explore the countryside. The Green Belt architects and campaigners halted the spread of the suburbs in the 1930s and 1940s, so true countryside can still be found close to London, even within the M25. Furthermore, England's train lines shoot out from the capital and make a large circle around London easily accessible for walking day trips. This ring is up to 140 miles in diameter, stretching from the border of Suffolk in the north to Beachy Head in the south and from the North Wessex Downs in the west to Broadstairs and Margate in the east. Captured within this circle are six areas of outstanding natural beauty, one national park and five national walking trails: Dedham Vale, the Chilterns, Kent Downs and Surrey Hills, the High Weald, North Wessex Downs, the South Downs National Park, the North Downs Way, the South Downs Way, the Thames Path, the Ridgeway and the England Coast path.

There's something very satisfying about treading the ground around London, like an animal walking the boundaries of its territory. As you follow these walks, you develop a sense of London located in a 3D topographical map. Bands of hills encircle London on three sides. Beyond lies the Vale of Aylesbury to the north and the undulating Weald to the south, then the South Downs rise up along the coast. The thick slick of the Thames slides through wide valleys to the west and expands into a tidal estuary beyond London, with creek-filled mudflats exposed at low tide.

Perhaps a predilection for the exotic in faraway places makes us less aware of what's remarkable closer to home. The White Cliffs of Dover, the dramatic end of the North Downs, display what is rare elsewhere in the world. Only a handful of other countries have similar outcrops of chalk. Made from the shells of microscopic algae, living in warm tropical seas over 60 million years ago, our chalk cliffs and downlands are extraordinary. Our ancient woodlands harbour more than half the world's bluebells, while the south-east remains England's most wooded region. Kent is still the Garden of England – boasting more orchards than other counties, totemic oast houses and the occasional hop field. The Thames Estuary is internationally important for the thousands of waders, geese and ducks that fly in for winter from Iceland, Siberia and Scandinavia. And then there's the opportunity to combine a walk with a day out in the cathedral city of Canterbury or one of several Victorian seaside towns.

Among this eulogising, notes of loss should also resonate. The past 50 years have seen unparalleled degradation of our landscape, sacrificed for profit and the drive for cheap food. Agribusiness has torn up hedges to create larger fields and industrial levels of chemical fertilisers, herbicides and pesticides have been used so intensively that wildflowers have been decimated and butterfly and other insect populations have collapsed. This in turn has led to a sharp decline in many farmland birds such as yellowhammers and corn buntings. I often see more birds in our London garden than in these agribusiness deserts. Our rivers have also been poisoned by runoff from fields doused in chemicals. Frighteningly, these losses may be insignificant compared to the damage climate change is starting to inflict.

On a more positive note, most of these walks weave through land protected by legislation or lovingly restored by green pioneers. It's heartening to see the efforts made to protect and improve what we have. While these oases haven't escaped damage, they allow a glimpse of the countryside we have lost and need to reinstate to help counteract the impact of climate change. Perhaps the more people explore and value our countryside, the more they will do to protect it and the more hope we will have.

Many people dream of moving out of London or to the country. But I wonder, do Londoners who develop a walking habit experience more countryside and a greater variety than those who have fled? Is their appreciation heightened because of the contrast with the city? As the walks in this book show, at least Londoners don't need a car to get there.

A NOTE ON DISTANCE, TIME, DIRECTIONS AND TRAINS

Distances are roughly measured using Ordnance Survey maps and rounded to half a mile. For various reasons the length registering on your apps may be longer. The time for each walk is based on a generous two miles per hour, so if you're a fast walker you'll complete the walk more quickly. Directions have been tested several times, but things change, signs disappear, hedges are pulled up, a stile may be replaced with a gate, and so on. To allow for this, the route for each walk is also drawn on an OS map. Train journeys can also change, or there might be a quicker route, so double-check before you set off.

Featured spring walks

1 Eridge Circular: early spring flowers
2 Chorleywood to Little Chalfont: celandines
3 Tring Circular: bluebells
4 Chartham to Canterbury: apple blossom
5 Penshurst to Leigh: cow parsley & hawthorn
6 Deal to Dover: seaside & chalkland flowers

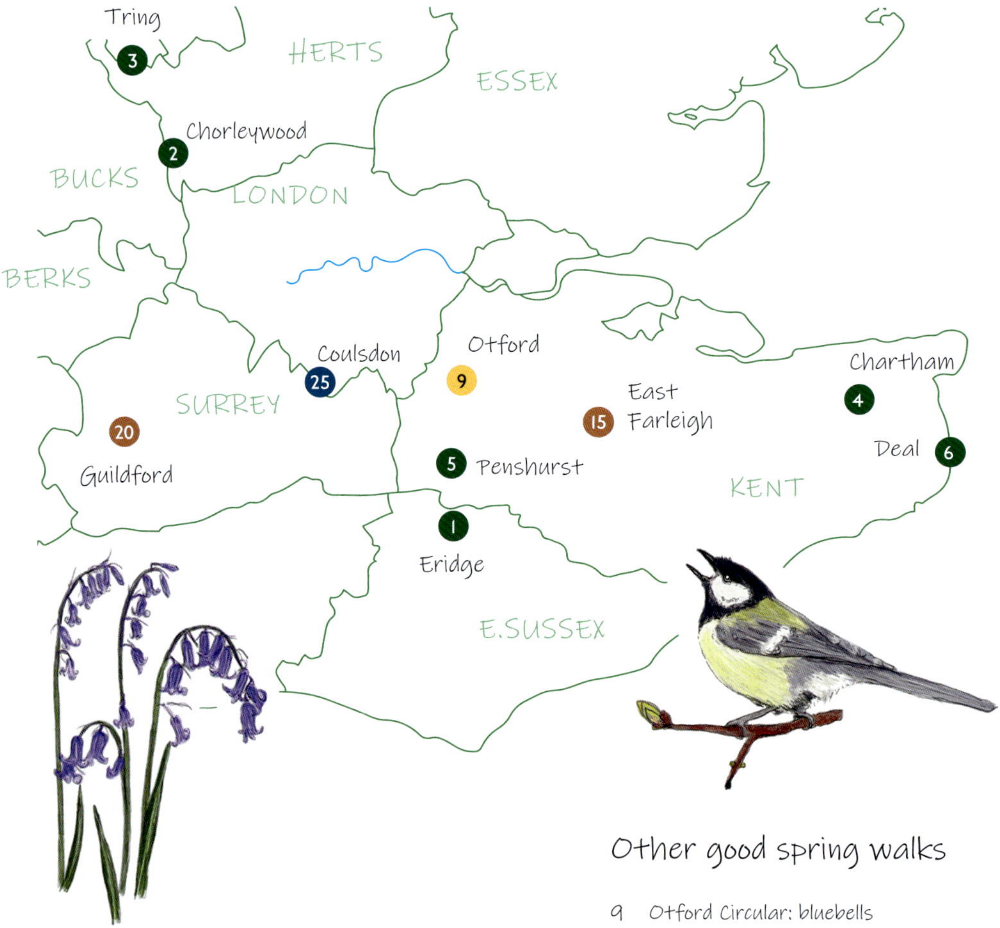

Other good spring walks

9 Otford Circular: bluebells
15 East Farleigh to Yalding: apple blossom
20 Guildford to Chilworth: bluebells
25 Coulsdon Circular: cowslips

SPRING

The world begins to smell again as the green scents of spring curl through the air. Birds break the silence of winter as they establish and defend their territories with song, and colour creeps back across the woodland floor.

But stride out in March or early April and you'll find that winter still has a hold on the landscape, providing a last chance to admire the intricate black skeletons of winter trees before they shake open their leaves.

Spring first shows in pockets: a clump of primroses, a patch of wood anemones, bleak winter hedgerows interrupted by blackthorn's fuzz of white blossom. Sunny days tempt peacock and brimstone butterflies out of hibernation, to dance sleepily along field edges.

But it's late April and early May I'm eager for, when the slow jog of early spring turns into a race. When bluebells try to beat the shade of the tree canopy, orchards explode with blossom and the countryside is suffused with the luminous light green of spring.

Everything seems to settle down in late spring. All our summer migrants have arrived, swallows dive low and swifts screech high above. The countryside is dressed in a froth of bridal white. Paths are edged with the lacy umbels of cow parsley, hawthorn trees are blurred by blossom and the flowers of wild garlic set about the woods like sparklers. The cordial smell of elderflowers heralds in May and replaces the sappy scents that infused early spring.

I've chosen 20 March, the spring equinox, as the start of 'walking spring'. Walks are staggered through the season, for early, mid and late spring. I've tried to find the best routes to enjoy bluebells, celandines, wood anemones and apple blossom. Trips included in the summer or autumn sections – which have bluebell woods, a profusion of other spring flowers or blossom – are referenced on the opposite page to give you a wider choice.

Wildflowers and blossom are the focus of these walks. However, among them you'll find places to enjoy newborn lambs, spring birdsong and butterflies, and there's an early trip to the seaside.

Timing is tricky. Flowering times vary from year to year and each display – perhaps most importantly its peak – tends to be short-lived. Apple blossom's fortnight of flowering can begin in the second week of April or the first week of May. So a specific weekend is recommended for several of these walks to give you the best chance of seeing a good display, even if in that year flowering is early or late.

Spring's beauty, exuberance and hope make it my favourite season. Perhaps it's the one season when it's worth reserving some dates in your diary for walking, so you don't miss its fleeting offerings.

ERIDGE CIRCULAR, EAST SUSSEX

A perfect stroll to kick-start walking after winter. Not too long, not too strenuous, but with plenty of early spring interest.

This walk is nestled in the High Weald Area of Outstanding Natural Beauty, a landscape little changed since medieval times. Rolling hills are covered with a patchwork of small irregular fields, most of which are meadows rather than given over to vegetables or arable crops. Fields are interspersed with small areas of woodland. Old scattered farmsteads are linked by winding roads bordered by hedges. This is the quintessential English countryside seen by those flying into Gatwick – the high planes at times slightly disturbing the tranquillity.

This exceptional area is out of bounds in winter because the Weald's clay becomes too wet and sticky, but towards the end of March it's usually dry enough to venture out. In contrast to the permeable chalklands of the Chilterns and North Downs, the sound of water seems ever present. Water gushes through steep-sided gills, over weirs and into pools.

This is a good walk to immerse yourself in spring birdsong. You'll hear the insistent repeated call of the chiffchaff recently arrived from the Mediterranean or West Africa. These little warblers used to be a first sign of spring. Things have changed. Now some overwinter in the UK although numbers are still swollen by migrants from March. Woods pulse with great tits' urgent squeaky bike call and the more melodious notes of wrens, robins and blackbirds. Great spotted woodpeckers tap out their territory and green woodpeckers laugh across meadows. At one point a long narrow field, bounded by sloping woods, becomes a magical tunnel of birdsong.

There is more road-walking on this route than I'd usually tolerate, but these are quiet country lanes with early spring flowers scattered along their verges. Damp ditches sprout

INFORMATION

BEST TIME: Last week of March or first week of April

LENGTH & DIFFICULTY: 6 miles (9.5km); easy but with several stiles

APPROXIMATE TIME: 3 hours

TRAINS: London Bridge to Eridge (Monday - Saturday hourly; 56 minutes). Longer on Sundays, when trains from Victoria with one change take 1¼ hours. Buy a day return to Eridge

MAP: OS Explorer 135 (Ashdown Forest)

FOOD & DRINK: Huntsman pub next to Eridge station (no food on Mondays, but open from 3pm)

PICNIC: Picnic tables four miles into the walk in Harrison's Rocks car park

TOILETS: Eridge station and four miles into the walk at Harrison's Rocks car park

cuckoo flowers, their pale lilac petals sitting on top of tall slender stems, white wood anemones settle on the shadier side and yellow stars of celandine rest on the grass. The arrow-shaped leaves of wild arum mix with hart's-tongue fern. While these verges don't quite boast a profusion of wildflowers, they give an inkling of what the countryside used to be like and are rich compared to verges in counties where herbicides and pesticides are used in higher volumes.

Blackthorn bushes sprout tiny pearl buds and small white flowers among their thorns; their blossom is at its height only for about 10 days, so easily missed.

The wood anemones found along the route are the reason this walk is featured. One of the first woodland flowers, their ice-white petals and clusters of yellow anthers sit on a bed of soft ferny leaves. It takes 100 years for wood anemones to advance six feet across a woodland floor, so woods where they thrive are probably ancient, visible on maps dating back to 1600 and therefore presumed to stretch back to prehistoric times. Few woods have these pretty flowers in any quantity, so their abundance in a couple of places along this walk is unusual.

The Weald seems to be the place I always return to for my first spring fix.

DIRECTIONS

1. Exit the station, turn right along the road and then take the first road on the right.

2. Continue along this winding road for 600m (ignore the turning to the Lodge and Hamilton House) and turn left along the second road, with a sign for Kentdale and signposted as a bridleway.

3. After about 1km (having ignored the turnoff to Motts Farm) stop following what has become a track when it bends to the right, rising up to a red brick house. Instead continue on the bridleway ahead, towards a gate.

4. Shortly after the gate across the path, turn right at a footpath post and walk over a footbridge. Walk up the hill.

5. At the top go through a kissing gate and continue straight on across four fields and downhill to meet and pass through a strip of woodland.

6. Go through a metal gate and continue ahead. Keep to the path (with the wood on your right), which you follow as it curves to the bottom of the hill. In the corner of the field, go through a gate and cross a footbridge over a stream.

7. Continue up through a wood, a field and over a stile onto a country road. Turn right along the road; in 500m you will reach the bottom of the hill.

8. Just before you cross the stream, turn left into Valley Cottage's parking area and pick up the footpath in the far right corner.

9. Continue for 800m, initially through a wood (ignore paths to the left) and then along a narrow field at the bottom of a valley.

10. Follow the footpath uphill through fields then down to the railway line and through the tunnel.

11. Cross small fields and a bridge to reach the road.

12. Turn left along the road, which will soon go uphill. In about 400m follow the road as it bends to the right and enters Groombridge.

13. Just before the school, turn right along a footpath alongside the school. Continue on the path until it ends at a road in about 400m.

14. Turn right along the road. Just before the road plunges downhill turn left onto a footpath by a line of tall pine trees.

15. At the bottom of the hill you reach a footpath junction with an information board and car park in front to your right. Continue on the path straight ahead, marked with a yellow footpath sign. Toilets and picnic benches can be found in the middle of the car park.

16. The path leads you through woods. When you emerge keep to the path next to the railway line, which in a while gives you good views of Harrison's Rocks, at a distance.

17. In around 800m the path ends at a gate; continue ahead to the oast house where you turn right

along the road and through a level crossing.

18. At the T-junction turn left and walk 1.5km along a quiet country road. When the road ends at a T-junction turn left to reach Eridge station. The pub is just beyond the station.

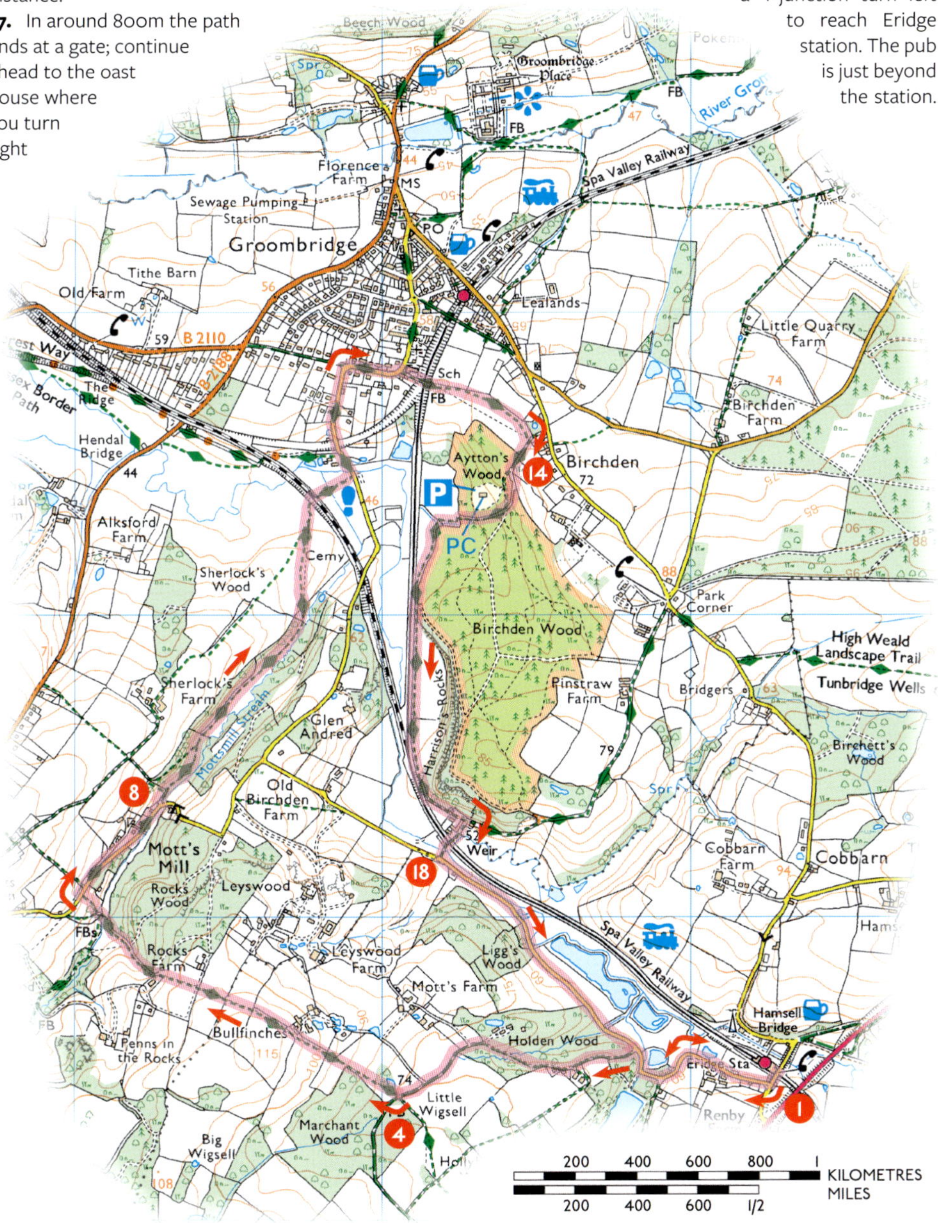

Walk 2

CHORLEYWOOD TO LITTLE CHALFONT, HERTFORDSHIRE AND BUCKINGHAMSHIRE

Celandines only grabbed my attention when I saw them completely covering a woodland floor.

These small yellow stars are an early spring flower and they erupt en masse on this walk from the end of March to mid-April, rising from a layer of tiny lily-pad leaves. Related to buttercups, their proper name is lesser celandine. Wordsworth's three poems about celandines aren't as famous as his elegies to daffodils, but he proclaimed these little spring messengers his favourite flower: "There's a flower that shall be mine, 'Tis the little Celandine". This walk along the Chess Valley in the Chilterns has been chosen because it takes in a beech wood carpeted with celandines. Satisfyingly, it starts at one Metropolitan line station and ends at another, with only a bit of road walking in between and this is along quiet residential streets. Just a few minutes from the station you are breathing in country air on Chorleywood Common, in another 10, you look down into the meadow-filled Chess Valley. Green fields curve down to the river, edged with the grey fur of winter trees. While most are empty, sheep, horses and even large white geese feed in others. Red kites circle above, skylarks fly up and you hear the distant yaffle of green woodpeckers. It all looks and feels very rural.

Early on you spy a corner of the M25 in the distance, but you're not disturbed by its noise for long. You drop down to the bottom of the valley to meet the River Chess. While you have a few sightings of this shallow chalk stream, alas there's no riverbank walking. Before you cross a weir over the Chess you pass the river's last remaining watercress farm, but it's a bit too early in the year to make a purchase. London's summer tables were supplied with watercress from this area in Victorian times, brought in by the newly constructed Metropolitan Railway.

INFORMATION

BEST TIME: A warm day in the first half of April
LENGTH & DIFFICULTY: 6½ miles (10.5km); moderate, with a couple of hills
APPROXIMATE TIME: 3¼ hours
TRAINS: Metropolitan line (frequent; 50 minutes from Kings Cross) or Marylebone station (twice an hour; 27 minutes) to Chorleywood. Return from Chalfont and Latimer to Marylebone or via the Metropolitan line. Both stations are in Transport for London zones, with Chalfont and Latimer the furthest in zone 8, so use contactless or your pass
MAP: OS Explorer 172 (Chiltern Hills East)
FOOD & DRINK: The Cock Inn, Church End (2 miles into the walk, closed Mondays) or Red Lion Chenies (4 miles into the walk)
PICNIC: A bench in Church End's churchyard or a bench with a view after the Chenies' celandine wood
TOILETS: At both stations

The walk passes through the village of Chenies and reaches the old brick facade of Chenies Manor, the remainder of a much larger Tudor dwelling and the location of Winston Churchill's house in the television series, *The Crown*.

The celandine wood is hidden at the end of an alley, bordered by brick and flint-napped walls, between the manor and the church. These tiny shiny flowers make a surprising impact at their peak. Arrive before late afternoon because they begin to shut as it becomes colder, and visit on a warmish day when the flowers should be fully open.

The walk ends with an easy stretch along the top of the valley and through more beechwoods before you make your way to the station along Little Chalfont's suburban roads. This is a well-known walk and deservedly so, although I'd describe it as scenic rather than spectacular, but nonetheless a very pleasant amble at the start of spring.

DIRECTIONS

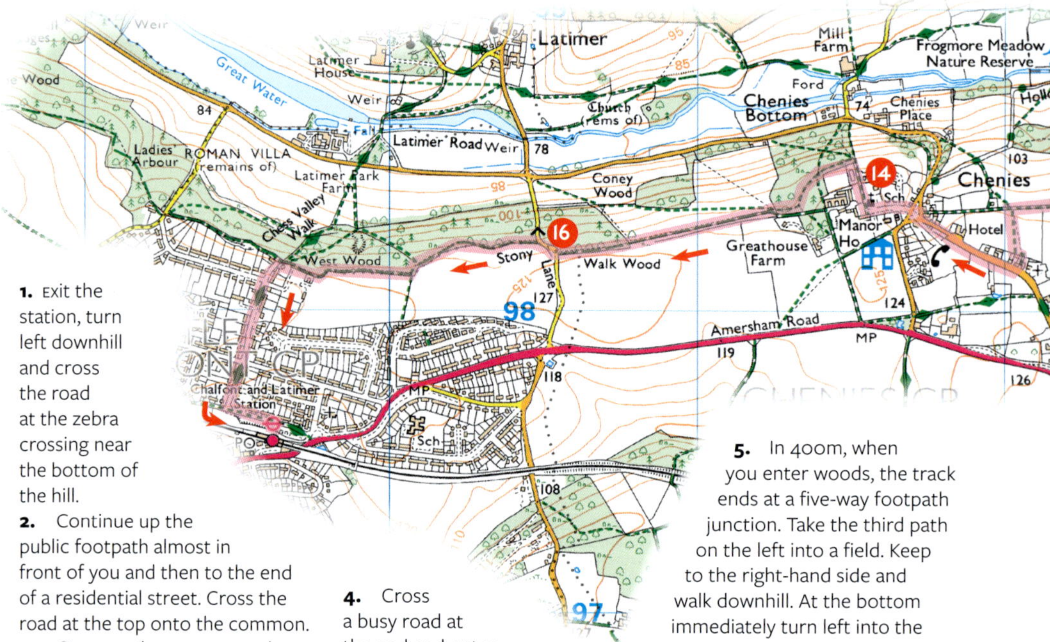

1. Exit the station, turn left downhill and cross the road at the zebra crossing near the bottom of the hill.

2. Continue up the public footpath almost in front of you and then to the end of a residential street. Cross the road at the top onto the common.

3. Once on the common, take the path that forks half-left, aiming for the tiled roofs. In about 400m, just after a clump of trees on your right, the path forks. Take the right fork and aim for a gap in the trees. Choose the left gap (with a white building at the end).

4. Cross a busy road at the end and enter Chorleywood House Estate along a tarmac drive. In about 300m, after you have entered the woods, turn right at the T-junction signposted to the River Chess. The path quickly forks; take the left fork.

5. In 400m, when you enter woods, the track ends at a five-way footpath junction. Take the third path on the left into a field. Keep to the right-hand side and walk downhill. At the bottom immediately turn left into the woods.

6. In about 400m, go through a gap in the fence and turn right to cross a footbridge over the River Chess. Keep to this footpath for another 600m (ignoring paths off to the right and cross a road halfway).

7. Follow the track as it sweeps round to the right, go through a wooden gate and uphill to a white house. Near the top pass through a kissing gate and then another, cross a tarmac drive and walk along the footpath ahead. Turn left into the churchyard.

8. Keeping the church on your right, exit the churchyard into a field. Turn left along the field boundary and cross two fields. Pass through a gate and continue ahead along a tree-lined path signposted to Dawes Lane.

9. In the next field follow the path diagonally across the field. Cross another field and on the other side go through a kissing gate and turn left down the road.

10. At the T-junction with Sarratt Bottom, turn right. When the road bends right, turn left along a drive, signposted to Latimer and continue for 500m until you reach a watercress farm. Just after the gate, turn left to cross the river.

11. Continue along the road. When it bends to the right, turn left onto a footpath, almost immediately turn right to follow the path uphill, signposted to Chenies Green. Keep to this path through the wood and eventually cross a field to Mountwood Farm ahead.

12. Go through the kissing gate and turn right along the footpath that becomes a road. In 350m turn left along the first footpath you come to.

13. Once in Chenies, turn right along the road, ideally on the grass verge then along the road. At the village green take the second road on the left to cross the green. Cross the road on the other side and walk ahead up the gravel drive until you reach the manor house (don't be put off by the private sign).

14. Turn right down a path between two walls. When you emerge into the celandine wood follow the path round to the left. In 400m exit the wood via a kissing gate.

15. Continue ahead for 800m until you reach a road. Initially you have valley views on your right and then you walk through another wood.

16. Cross the road and turn right downhill. In about 100m turn left along a bridleway signposted Chilterns Cycle Way. Keep at the same height. In 400m turn left at a footpath T-junction and walk towards a playing field, seen through a gap in the hedge. Just before the field, turn right and continue along the path just inside the wood.

17. In 400m (after passing the playing field and then a car park) at an intersection of five paths, with a garden fence on your left, turn left into Chalfont and along a residential road.

18. At the crossroads walk ahead down Chenies Avenue until you come to a T-junction. Turn left along Bedford Avenue. In 200m go through the gap in the fence and up to the station.

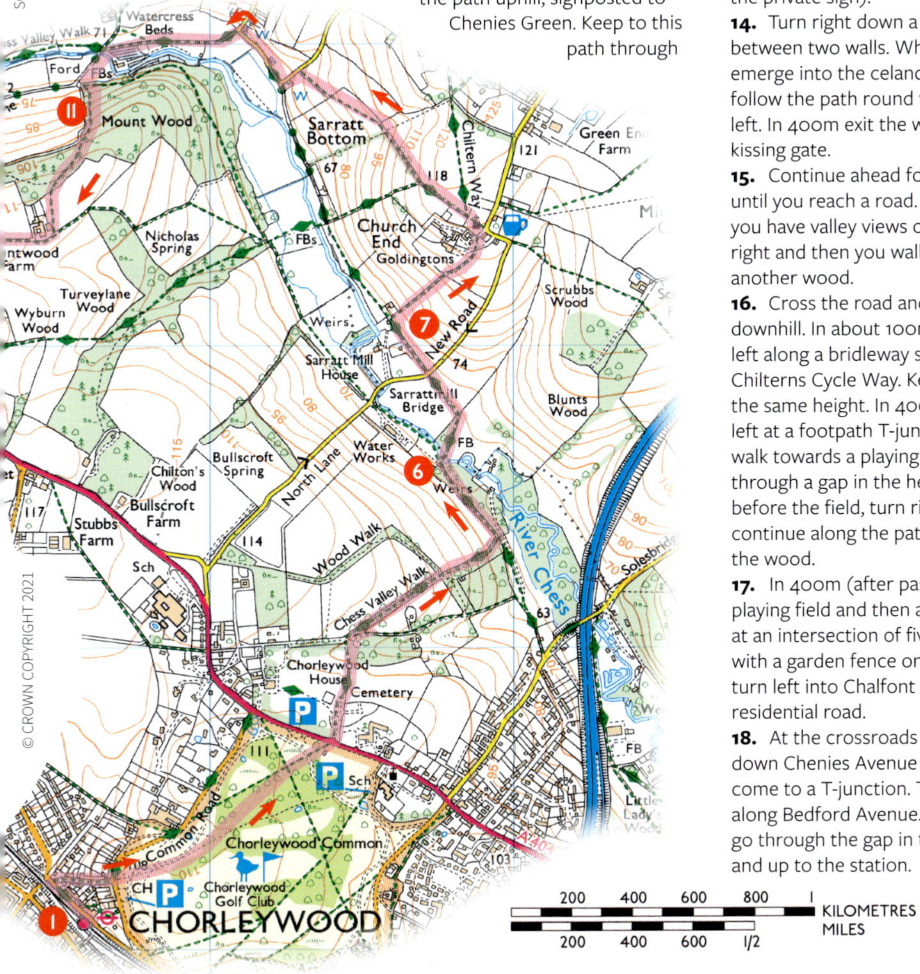

SCALE 1:25 000 OR 2½ INCHES TO 1 MILE 4CM TO 1 KM

Walk 3

TRING CIRCULAR, HERTFORDSHIRE AND BUCKINGHAMSHIRE

A magnificent hike along the Chilterns chalk escarpment, followed by a wander around Ashridge Estate's Dockey Wood.

This walk, only 40 minutes from Euston, is one of my favourites. The route is pretty stunning throughout with lots of variety and a surfeit of nature. At the end I always feel it's been a day well spent.

There are two options: the shorter version misses out Ivinghoe Beacon. Both have little road walking. After leaving Tring station the route quickly joins the Ridgeway, reputedly the oldest road in Britain – now a long-distance path that starts in Wiltshire and ends here, 87 miles later, on this walk at Ivinghoe Beacon.

In late April the tree canopy is a haze of backlit limelight, so the early stretch under the beech hanger of Aldbury Nowers is particularly delightful. Then suddenly you're striding along the exposed ridge of Pitstone Hill with wide views over to Ivinghoe Beacon. There's a tremendous sense of openness and space. After human-sized London I always feel pleasantly small and insignificant.

These hills are marked by people from prehistory: traces of an Iron Age fort on Ivinghoe Beacon and the path along Pitstone Hill runs along the bank of Grim's Ditch, a Bronze Age network of boundary dykes. Signs of old field systems, medieval flint mines, burial mounds and herders' tracks can be found along the walk if you know what to look for.

Cowslips with their small sprays of egg yolk flowers dot the downland and increase in number until they form a long drift through a field of dandelions. Skylarks rise singing from the rough grass and then suddenly drop, like animatronic birds moving up and down invisible wires. Gorse, its pea-like flowers smelling of coconut, is in bloom at the top.

Keep an eye out for fallow deer, some may be descendants from the royal deer park at Ashridge – established in the

INFORMATION

BEST TIME: Last week in April

LENGTH & DIFFICULTY: Main walk 10.5 miles (17km), shorter option 9 miles (14.5km), the shortcut is blue on the map; moderate, with three steep hills on the main walk and two on the shorter

APPROXIMATE TIME: Main walk 5¼ hours. Shorter option 4½ hours

TRAINS: Euston to Tring (Monday to Saturday four an hour, Sunday hourly; from 35 minutes). Buy a day return to Tring

MAP: OS Explorer 181 (Chiltern Hills North)

FOOD & DRINK: Near the end, National Trust cafe next to the Bridgewater Monument or in Aldbury; the Trooper (Wed - Sun), the Barn (Tues-Sun until 3pm), the Greyhound Inn

PICNIC: On Pitstone Hill or the hills around Ivinghoe Beacon. Benches near Aldbury Nowers and at the top of the escarpment (direction 8)

TOILETS: No toilets at Tring station. National Trust toilets near Bridgewater Monument close to the end

13th century and one of the first. While fallow deer were first introduced to Britain by the Romans, it's thought the Normans brought them here. The muntjac deer are more solitary and easily mistaken for hares or dogs as they creep through the woods. At Ashridge, as elsewhere, there has been an explosion in the deer population, which grew fivefold in 40 years. More recently the Estate has organised a larger deer cull to reduce the devastating effect they were having on trees, other wildlife, plants and fungi.

When you reach the Beacon, panoramic views extend across Buckinghamshire and into Oxfordshire and along the Chiltern ridge in either direction. Fires are lit here to mark national events and because it's close to Elstree Studios, the Beacon apparently features in *The Avengers*, *The Saint*, *Harry Potter* and *Star Wars*.

There's more ridge walking along a spur off the Beacon towards Gallows Hill, with views to Dunstable Downs and a chalk lion carved into the hillside, the largest hill figure in England, marks Whipsnade Zoo. As you descend the ridge, you leave open downland behind and make your way to Ward's Hurst Farm, where newborn lambs fill the fields, now and again jumping in joyous spasms. Then it's into woods full of birdsong.

The smallish, fenced-in Dockey Wood is overwhelmed with bluebell tourists at weekends, but it's spectacular and a good place to catch the flower's shifting scent. These delicate arched beauties thrive under the dense beech canopies of the Chilterns, which suppress the growth of competing plants. Like wood anemones, they are a key indicator species of ancient woodland. In the past arrows were set with their sticky sap, books were bound and Elizabethan ruffs starched.

The walk continues through woodland filled with birdsong and ends in the picturesque village of Aldbury with its pubs, duck pond, stocks and whipping post. A shortish walk across fields returns you to Tring station. Few walks are as satisfying as this.

DIRECTIONS

1. At Tring station walk up the stairs and turn right. Then turn left alongside the car park to reach the road and turn right along the road.

2. Cross over the car park entrance and almost immediately go through a kissing gate in the hedge on your right. Turn left and in about 200m, when the hedge ends, cross the road and go straight ahead up a path signposted Ridgeway.

3. Turn left at a footpath crossroads marked with a four-armed signpost. From here just follow Ridgeway signposts (sometimes only marked with an acorn – the symbol of Britain's National Trails) until the long-distance path ends at Ivinghoe Beacon, 5km away. In more detail:

4. Walk along the tree-lined path. Turn right uphill, past Aldbury Nowers information board. Ignore a footpath on the left, after which you turn left up a flight of steps. After the stairs, veer left (as directed by the footpath sign) along the wooded hillside for almost 1km until you emerge onto the open downland ridge of Pitstone Hill.

5. Continue ahead along the hillside. After around 1km, near the bottom of the hill, take the middle path to go around the high mound.

6. Walk through the car park, cross the road and continue ahead. Keep to the main path as you climb to the top of the escarpment.

7. At the top, when you come to a gate, don't go through it but follow the path to the left of the gate and continue ahead. For the longer walk continue from point **13**.

8. **For the shorter option** (the shortcut is coloured blue on the map) follow the line of gorse and at the bench, turn right and go through a kissing gate. Continue ahead through woodland and across a car park (which the National Trust may block off). Cross the road and walk through a line of trees to join a footpath, running along the hillside.

9. Turn right along this path; when you emerge into an area of grassland (which has been used as a car park) continue in the same direction, aiming for a wooden post on the other side.

10. When you reach the post, pass through a gate and take the footpath on the left, which takes you along the edge of the escarpment.

11. After around 1km, the path will fork and later forks again; each time take the higher right fork.

12. When the path ends at a T-junction, with a field in front, turn right and at the gate pick up the main walk at **20** below.

13. **For the longer option**, continue ahead, ignoring paths off to the left and right, aiming for the dark footpath post. Continue into the woods. Follow the path downhill to a road.

DIRECTIONS

Beacon Hill
Ivinghoe Hills
Town Farm
Ridgeway
Icknield Way Trail
Steps Hill
Incombe Hole
The Coombe
Ward's Coombe
Hanging Coombe
Ward's Hurst Farm
Crawley Wood
Ringshall Coppice
Dockey Wood
Brook's Stath Wood
Clipper Down
Duncombe Terrace
Beacon Road
Down Farm
Ivinghoe Common
Reservoir
Pitstone Hill
Duncombe Farm
Barley End
Flat Isley
Hanging Isley
Golding's Spring
Aldbury Nowers
Grim's Ditch
Moneybury Hill
Sallow Copse
Tim's Spring
Walk Wood
Howlett's Wood
Pitstone Common
Stocks Golf Club
Stock's Farm
Little Stocks
Bridgewater Monument
Aldbury
Westland Farm
Hertfordshire Way
Church Farm
Station Road
Tring Station
Aldbury Common
Thunderdell Cottages
Prince's R
KILOMETRES
MILES

14. Cross the road and follow the footpath that forks left up to Ivinghoe Beacon.

15. At Ivinghoe Beacon turn right and walk along Beacon Hill ridge. Pass through the first kissing gate. When you reach the second kissing gate (initially out of view) turn right downhill.

16. Go through a field gate at the bottom. Walk the short distance to a line of trees and take the path on the right, crossing the field towards a hill.

17. Go through a gate and turn left. When the path splits, take the left fork following the line of trees (on your left) forming the field boundary; this will eventually bring you to a kissing gate that leads into woodland.

18. Go through the gate. In 600m you come to a large wooden post. Now turn right into a pine wood.

19. Follow the footpath signs through the wood. You emerge from the top left corner of the wood. The path then leads you up a flight of steps.

20. Pass through the gate and follow the footpath across a field. Go through another gate into the farmyard, walk ahead and go through the gate on the other side.

21. Walk straight ahead to cross the field (usually full of lambs). In the second field, at a three-armed footpath post, turn right and walk along the edge of the field. In the next field, cross the field diagonally, aiming for the gate in the far left corner.

22. Once through the gate, cross the road and turn left along the verge. You come to the car park entrance. Opposite is the entrance to Dockey Wood.

23. After exploring the wood, retrace your steps. Cross the road and turn right along the verge. Take the footpath on the right (just after Dockey Wood ends), diagonally across the field. Then turn right along the hedge.

24. At the footpath T-junction, turn right. Follow the footpath for about 1km across fields, and then turn right at the end of woodland and head downhill to a road.

25. Pick up the footpath across the road, slightly to the right. Continue ahead for about 350m.

26. When a footpath joins from the right, follow the footpath as it bends sharply left.

27. At the footpath T junction turn right. When you reach an another T junction, in a larger clearing, turn left.

28. At the next footpath crossroads, turn right (if you continued ahead you'd reach a road).

29. Follow this path for 1km until you reach another footpath crossroads. Turn right, signposted to the visitor centre.

30. When you reach the drive, turn right and follow the drive round to the left and then quickly right towards the National Trust visitor centre.

31. Walk past the cafe and past a multiple armed signpost on the right. Continue ahead downhill.

32. Ignore a right turnoff and later a left turnoff. Later take the right fork.

33. At the bottom turn right onto the road to reach the village green.

34. To return to Tring station make your way ahead to the church, then walk along the road until you reach a footpath on the left, just before the road bends.

35. Once through the gate, immediately turn right and follow the field hedges, with the road just the other side, for about 1.5km until you reach the kissing gate in the hedge. The gate leads you onto the road, turn left to reach Tring station.

Walk 4

CHARTHAM TO CANTERBURY, KENT

The Garden of England is being dug up – 85 percent of Kent's orchards have been lost in the past 50 years.

So venture out this spring to savour the remains of this precarious, precious spectacle. Disappointment too often characterised my walks to see blossom. I thought I'd planned a brilliant route, only to discover it didn't wind through orchards but was funnelled along paths with high hedges completely obscuring the trees I'd come to see. So this walk purposely leads you into the heart of Newmafruit's orchards: acres of pear and apple orchards full of conference, comice, braeburn, cox, russet, gala and spartan. These are industrial orchards with line upon line of short, high-yield trees. But they still have a wow factor. There are thousands of them. As you move through you catch their elusive perfume. Before you reach the trees, you pass row upon row of static caravans, home to the army of pickers.

But the highlight is stumbling upon No Man's Orchard along the North Downs Way, now a community orchard, full of widely spaced, mature fruit trees topped with broad canopies of blossom. No Man's Orchard is now classed as organic; no sprays have been used since 1993. It's a haven for wildlife, full of birdsong and the occasional darting woodpecker, and was the first orchard to become a designated nature reserve. The contrast with the insecticide-drenched commercial orchards – wildlife deserts with only the occasional bird – is stark.

Most of the apples here are Bramleys, but Howgate Wonders, James Grieve and Worcesters were planted as pollinators. Many traditional orchards are lost because dying trees are not replaced, but this orchard is now being replenished. To expand it, cider apple trees were planted in 1996 and more recently the Flower of Kent and Kentish

INFORMATION

BEST TIME: Blossoms' peak varies, but best bet is the last week of April
LENGTH & DIFFICULTY: Main walk 8 miles (13km), shorter option 5 miles (8km) the shortcut is in blue on the map; easy, both are reasonably flat but have several stiles
APPROXIMATE TIME: Main walk 4 hours. Shorter option 2½ hours
TRAINS: St Pancras to Chartham changing at Ashford (hourly; 1 hour 5 minutes), Charing Cross (hourly; 1 hour 38 minutes). Return from Canterbury West to St Pancras (hourly; 1 hour), Charing Cross (hourly, 1 hour 49 minutes). From Canterbury East to Victoria (from hourly; 1 hour 34 minutes). Buy a day return to Canterbury
MAP: OS Explorer 150 (Canterbury)
FOOD & DRINK: Plenty of places in Canterbury
PICNIC: Canterbury's Westgate Gardens or No Man's Orchard on the main walk; both have benches
TOILETS: Chartham Village Hall car park, then none until you reach Canterbury

Fillbasket – more traditional apple varieties – have replaced trees that have died.

You're free to wander among the twisted old trees, passing pastel drifts of cuckoo flowers thriving in the long grass. This is how orchards used to be. The benches around the perimeter offer several good picnic spots.

Perhaps the movement to plant and revitalise community orchards is the only sure way of passing down the pleasure of spring blossom to future generations, while creating little oases of nature.

But this walk isn't all about orchards. It begins with a riverside walk along the Great Stour, a fast-flowing chalk river, which you rejoin as you walk into Canterbury. More than 85 percent of the world's rare chalk streams are found in England, their implausibly clear water the result of slow filtering through calcareous rock. Finally, you can explore the UNESCO World Heritage site of Canterbury.

On the short version you'll have the pleasure of the riverside walk and half your time will be spent in orchards, albeit the industrial ones (you'll miss out on No Man's Orchard).

DIRECTIONS

1. Exit the station at the end of platform 2 by the signal box and turn left across the level crossing. Continue along the road past the village playing field.

2. After the village hall car park turn left along the Great Stour Walk footpath for 2km until you meet the A28. As you approach the A road, don't follow the footpath as it bends left; instead walk up a small embankment and go through a kissing gate.

3. Turn left along the road and continue on the pavement as it bends left. In 250m, when you see the signpost to Chartham Hatch turn right up Howfield Lane.

4. In 200m, with an obscured footpath post on your right, turn right down the side of a warehouse and turn left behind the warehouse (the route of the footpath). After an oil store turn right along a car-wide track. Go past the caravans to reach the orchards.

5. **For the short walk** continue for about 1km until you reach a lane. Turn right to walk down this lane and pick up instruction **18** on the main walk, but turn right down the lane. The shortcut is in blue on the map.

6. **For the longer walk**, in 400m turn left up another car-wide track (the second you come to). Walk under the railway bridge and follow the path round to the right.

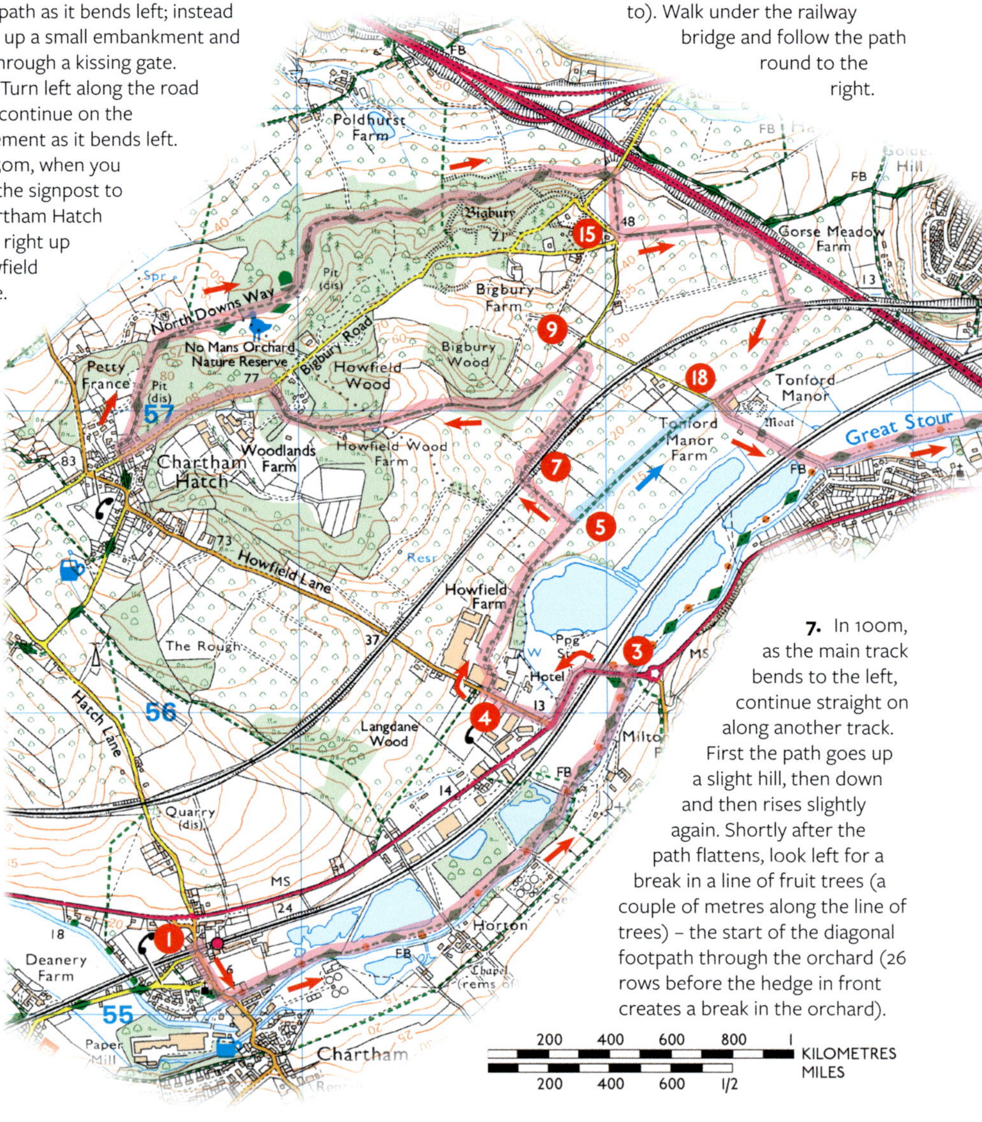

7. In 100m, as the main track bends to the left, continue straight on along another track. First the path goes up a slight hill, then down and then rises slightly again. Shortly after the path flattens, look left for a break in a line of fruit trees (a couple of metres along the line of trees) – the start of the diagonal footpath through the orchard (26 rows before the hedge in front creates a break in the orchard).

If you come to a high hedge on your left with an oak tree a little way in you have come too far, but you can pick up the stile if you turn left, keeping the hedge on your right – the stile is on the right almost at the end).

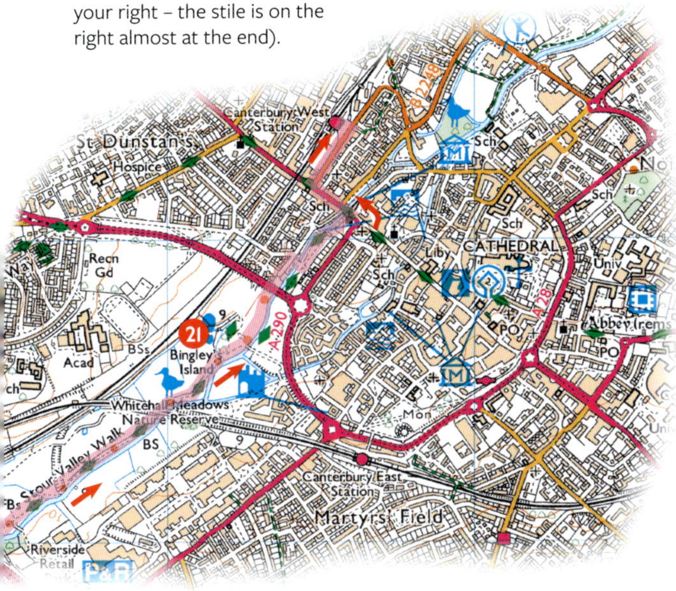

8. Climb over the stile in the hedge ahead, into another orchard and continue along another diagonal path through the orchard. At the end, climb over the stile in the hedge ahead, but slightly to the right.

9. Turn left along a fenced-in bridleway. In 800m this becomes the driveway to Little Howfield Wood Farm.

10. Walk on until you reach a T-junction with a road. Turn left onto the road and in 400m you reach Chartham Hatch.

11. After a few houses turn right at the tall post on the left, with footpath markers. Take the right fork into a playing field. After the playground follow the path next to the fence.

12. In 400m you come to No Man's Orchard. Almost at the end of the orchard go through a gate on the left into the woods.

13. In about 600m, pass through a gate next to Blean Woodlands information board. Later when you go through another gate turn right.

14. Continue along the path until you come to a road, go straight across, leaving the North Downs Way. Walk up a few steps, climb over the stile and continue ahead along a path with a tall field hedge on your left. At the end of the field bear left and pass through a gap next to a stile on your right.

15. Turn left down a bridleway (which skirts a large area of orchard), at one point coming close to the A2. In 400m you emerge into a field. Follow the yellow footpath marker and walk downhill to the bottom of the field.

16. Turn left along the bottom. When you come to a step stile on your right (about a third of the way along), climb over and carefully cross the train track.

17. Follow the direction of the yellow footpath marker on the step, half right, diagonally through the orchard. Don't doubt yourself and keep going until you reach the field margin, where you pass through the fence, then turn right along the footpath.

18. In 150m you arrive at a junction with a lane, turn left to walk down the lane.

19. In 400m cross the railway line and continue ahead to the T-junction at the River Stour.

20. Turn left along the footpath to follow the river, (the Stour Valley Walk). In around 2km you reach a playground (not long after you've passed under an arched railway bridge).

21. The path forks at the playground; keep right following signs to the city centre. Ignore a path to the right across a bridge. Instead keep straight ahead signposted to Westgate Gardens and Riverside Walk.

22. Pass under a road and enter Westgate Gardens. Turn right over the first bridge then turn left, to keep next to the river until you exit the park, with Medieval Westgate in front of you.

23. To return to London via Canterbury West, turn left along St Dunstans Street. The second right leads to the station.

24. If you want to explore Canterbury turn right and cross the road at the pedestrian crossing around the corner. Turn left and then right along St Peter's Street to enter pedestrianised medieval Canterbury. The cathedral is further down on the left.

Walk 5

PENSHURST TO LEIGH, KENT

Does the countryside you're exposed to as a child become the landscape of your heart?

Imprinted on mine are the quiet valleys filled with ancient woodland, undulating hills and endless small pastures of the High Weald. So while other walks may have more magnificent displays of hawthorn blossom and cow parsley, on this ramble you'll wander through pretty Weald countryside and still be delighted by hedgerows filled with small white flowers and edged with the froth of cow parsley.

What's more, step off the train at Penshurst station (which confusingly is in Chiddingstone Causeway, not Penshurst) and a minute later you're striding across fields. Initially you walk in the flatter Low Weald before crossing into the High Weald, a landscape hardly changed since the 14th century. The High Weald has one of the highest concentrations of isolated early farmsteads in Europe, mainly dating from the 1700s or earlier, so you frequently stumble across timber-framed houses and barns, with steep, wavy, red tiled roofs, weatherboard exteriors and hanging clay tiles. The rich network of footpaths and country roads represent old drovers' paths, used to drive livestock to pannage, to feed on acorns and beech mast in autumn, or transhumance, shifting livestock onto pasture appropriate for the season.

In May clouds of cow parsley bloom along country lanes. Its abundance is a result of unnaturally high nitrogen levels in the soil, primarily due to the use of fertilisers. The profusion of cow parsley is double edged – it is breathtaking, but it squeezes out less robust species of wildflower.

Cow parsley also flourishes in the semi shade of the hedgerows, which in the Weald tend to be a mixture of blackthorn, hazel, field maple and hawthorn. The hawthorn in the hedgerows comes into flower at the same time as cow

INFORMATION

BEST TIME: Second to fourth week in May
LENGTH & DIFFICULTY: 8½ miles (14km); moderate, short climbs and lots of stiles
APPROXIMATE TIME: 4¼ hours
TRAINS: London Bridge to Penshurst, one change (Mon-Sat twice an hour, Sunday hourly; from 49 minutes), buy a day return to Penshurst. Return from Leigh to London Bridge (hourly; 46 minutes)
MAP: OS Explorer 147 (Sevenoaks and Tonbridge)
FOOD & DRINK: In Chiddingstone; The Tulip Tree Tea Room (9am–5pm) and The Castle Inn. In Penshurst; Fir Tree House Tea Rooms (Wednesday to Sunday 2–5pm) and The Leicester Arms
PICNIC: Benches in the vineyard (direction 22) and at Penshurst's church
TOILETS: No toilets

parsley, but while pleasing, it can't compete with the beauty of mature hawthorn trees in blossom (which alas don't feature on this walk). These trees are often referred to as May trees or simply May. The old adage "Ne'er cast a clout till May be out" warns against discarding winter clothes until warmth is more certain. The May probably refers to hawthorn rather than the month, as its eruption into blossom – delayed if the weather is cold – heralds summer.

You'll notice the once neat, thick, tangled hedges have been neglected, the shrubs have thinned, grown tall or died, leaving sparse, gappy hedgerows that no longer provide ideal shelter or abundant food for wildlife. Thankfully, the High Weald Area of Outstanding Natural Beauty is encouraging landowners to restore their hedges through coppicing and hedge-laying. Another feature of this area is the partitioning of pastures by thick strips of mature deciduous trees known as shaws.

As you wander along, you'll dip down into wooded gills, with a stream winding along the bottom. The steep slopes of one gill are covered in waves of wild garlic. From the meadows on the hills, there are views across to the Greensand Ridge with the tops of oast houses poking above the trees.

Along the route you'll also have the pleasure of passing through the historic villages of Chiddingstone and Penshurst, each with a pleasant pub. My favourite tea room, Fir Tree House Tea Rooms, can be found in Penshurst. The walk ends with a long ramble through the parkland of Penshurst Place, established as a medieval deer park in the 14th century. A long ridge walk gives you views north and south before you descend to Leigh station.

DIRECTIONS

1. At the end of platform one exit the station (ignore the footbridge) and turn right to walk across the concrete. Pick up the footpath to the left of the gate.

2. Follow the footpath across two fields and then as it swings left and through a metal gate.

3. Cross the next field and climb over a stile – you'll see an old farmstead in the distance. A third of the way along the next field, turn left to climb over another stile.

4. Again cross this field. A few metres after you pass through a line of trees in front of you, go through the gate on your right.

5. Continue ahead to cross the field, then go through a gate and over a wooden bridge.

6. You then aim for the left side of the house on the hill. To get there, once over the bridge continue half-left, aiming for the footpath post. Once at the post walk uphill (with hedge on your left). When you come to a large break in the hedge, walk up to the house; turn right just after the house.

7. At the end of the drive, cross the road, follow the footpath across the field and go through a gap in the hedge.

8. Continue ahead and follow the path as it bends left. Keep going until the footpath ends at a gate on the right at the bottom of the hill.

9. Turn left along the footpath, which soon passes over the River Eden. A little later, at the footpath signpost, take the path on the right (diagonally across the

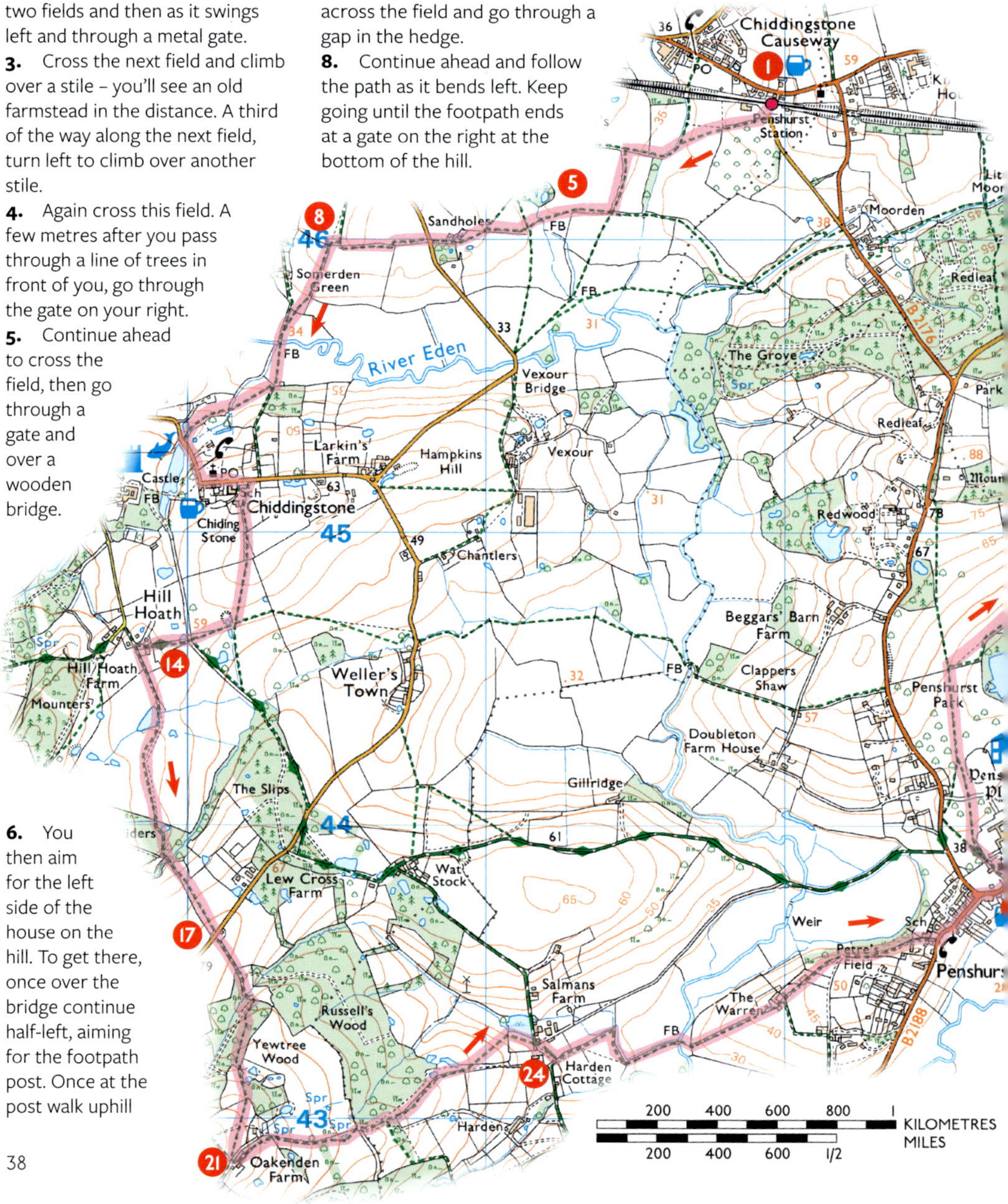

field to the far right corner and through a strip of trees into the next field) which in 400m ends at a road.

10. Turn left to walk into Chiddingstone and follow the road as it bends left.

11. As you're about to leave the village, just after a small green with a bench, turn right along a footpath. In 250m (after passing a playing field on your left) you emerge into a field.

12. Continue downhill. A few metres after a wood appears on your right, turn into the wood through a kissing gate.

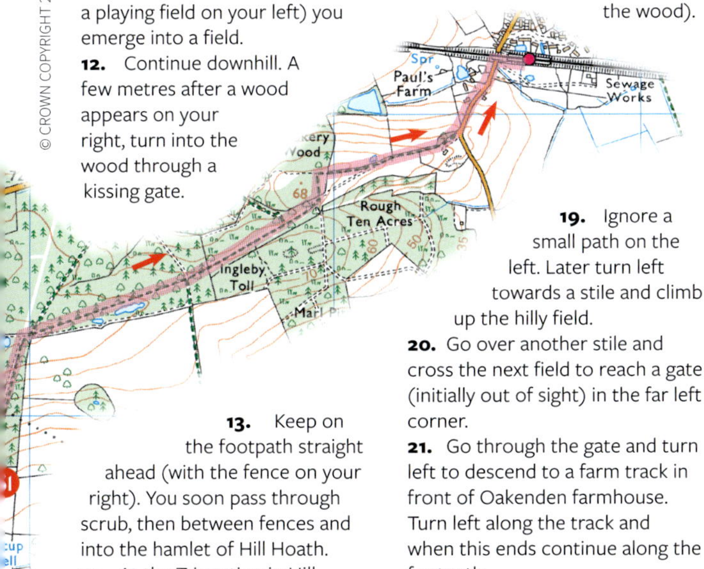

13. Keep on the footpath straight ahead (with the fence on your right). You soon pass through scrub, then between fences and into the hamlet of Hill Hoath.

14. At the T-junction in Hill Hoath, turn left along a farm track between a weeping willow and stables.

15. Keep on the footpath as it passes a pond and then crosses a field. Halfway across the field a hedge appears; continue in the same direction, keeping the hedge on your left until you enter a wood.

16. Follow the path as it bears right, down into a valley (ignore a field gate on the right) and up again. As you emerge from the wood, take the left fork, go through a kissing gate and climb uphill to the road.

17. Turn right along the road. In a few metres turn left through a kissing gate.

18. Walk along the farm track. At the end climb over a stile to the right of a field gate. When you reach a gravel area, find the footpath straight ahead, which takes you downhill and then uphill through a wood and then along the top (still in the wood).

19. Ignore a small path on the left. Later turn left towards a stile and climb up the hilly field.

20. Go over another stile and cross the next field to reach a gate (initially out of sight) in the far left corner.

21. Go through the gate and turn left to descend to a farm track in front of Oakenden farmhouse. Turn left along the track and when this ends continue along the footpath.

22. In around 400m climb over a stile. Later when the path bears right, turn left along a footpath over a ditch, which takes you along the top of a vineyard.

23. Then follow the footpath as it winds through fields and eventually downhill to a hamlet.

24. Walk ahead along the road for a few metres and turn right along a bridleway. When the track bends right, turn left down a footpath.

25. Follow this path as it winds through fields for about 1km (passing over the River Eden again on the way) until it becomes a road between cottages and an allotment. Continue on this road to Penshurst.

26. Turn left along Penhurst's main road. Ignore the first road on the left (although Fir Tree House Tea Rooms is just along here) and continue until you reach a courtyard of old houses, with a flat arch at the end. You may want to criss-cross the main road to keep on pavements.

27. Turn into the courtyard and walk under the arch, past the church and into parkland.

28. Continue ahead past Penshurst Place. Shortly after the footpath post, ignore a right fork. Continue ahead passing fir trees on the right.

29. Cross the driveway and continue ahead between rows of trees. At the end of the cricket pitch on the right, follow the path as it bears right through the trees, and then continue in the same direction, keeping the large oak to your right.

30. When you come to a metal kissing gate, go through it and turn right towards the clipped yew bushes.

31. Aim for the gate ahead (initially out of sight) then take the path half-left uphill, past the ancient tree trunk.

32. Continue uphill along a ride. At the top of the hill turn right at the footpath post.

33. Keep on this path, along the ridge, for 1.5km until it ends at a road. Initially there's a lengthy stretch along an avenue of trees. When the path eventually bends to the left continue ahead across a field.

34. The path ahead then follows a fence on the left until you eventually descend to the road.

35. Turn left along the road and you'll soon see the station.

SCALE 1:25 000 OR 2½ INCHES TO 1 MILE 4CM TO 1 KM

DEAL TO DOVER, KENT

A superb late spring seaside walk, which is also very straightforward. Just follow the coastal path from Deal to Dover.

It begins with classic English seaside without the brash and ends with an exhilarating walk along the clifftops. Don't let the length put you off. The route is easy to follow, with surprisingly few big ups and downs and there are plenty of reasons to stop and rest on the way. Long May days allow you to take your time.

The short walk is there and back from the station to the Zetland Arms pub.

Five minutes after leaving Deal Station you suddenly come to the sea, a simple pier before you and neat rows of higgledy-piggledy Georgian houses behind. This is seaside on a small scale. Compact fishing boats rear up from the shingle beach, each surrounded by a jumble of lobster pots, nets, flagged buoys and rope, mixed up with the primary colours of plastic crates. You catch that seaside whiff.

As you walk on, flowers begin to colonise the beach. Miles of clumped white, pink and red valerian are later joined by swathes of ox-eye daisies. Along here, I can't resist picking out the villa for my fantasy seaside life, nor can I resist stopping at the Zetland Arms, a pub on the beach, for a bit of contemplation before the cliff ascent. For those who like a sea dip, the water is now a decent temperature for swimming either off Deal beach or at St Margaret's Bay at high tide.

Up on the cliffs downland flowers colour your way. Pink sainfoin runs through the grass, accompanied by the yellow gorse-like flowers of bird's-foot trefoil. The blue of common milkwort may catch your eye, a strange combination of minuscule white stars and grain-like petals. Clumps of yellow kidney vetch remind me of tiny cowslips.

At times the air is full of birdsong. Invisible skylarks spill out their tuneful distortion of trills, conspicuous

INFORMATION

BEST TIME: Last week of May
LENGTH & DIFFICULTY: 11 miles (17.5km); moderate, one steep climb and descent and other ups and downs. Shorter walk 6 miles (9.5km); easy
APPROXIMATE TIME: Main walk 5½ hours. Shorter walk 3 hours
TRAINS: St Pancras to Deal (twice an hour; from 1 hour 25 minutes). Return from Dover Priory to St Pancras (hourly; 1 hour 5 minutes), or to Victoria, one change (hourly; 1 hour 40 minutes), or to Charing Cross direct (weekdays twice an hour, weekends hourly; 2 hours). Buy a day return to Dover Priory
MAP: OS Explorer 138 (Dover)
FOOD & DRINK: Zetland Arms on the beach
5km into the walk, the Coastguard pub or kiosk at St Margaret's Bay, restaurants or take-aways in Dover
PICNIC: Benches along the clifftop
TOILETS: At both stations, Walmer and Dover seafront and St Margaret's Bay

yellowhammers broadcast their classic 'little bread and no cheese' lament and posses of linnets warble, their breasts flushed with pink. The sun coaxes out fritillaries and the rare Adonis Blue, one of several species of blue butterfly that thrive here.

St Margaret's Bay, the closest you'll get to France in the UK, provides a welcome interlude. A kiosk sells quality ice-cream and there's a pub. A gorgeous walk along the White Cliffs of Dover follows. Now and again a huge white buttress rises up in front – usually with some brave soul standing close to the edge; the decision to put nothing between the path and cliff edge has to be admired. Towards the end of the walk is a bird's-eye view of shabby Dover Port, the busiest ferry port in Europe, with its noise and trails of lorries. The walk ends with a stroll along Dover's seafront, before you head into town to catch the train.

1. Turn right out of Deal station and then left along Albion Place.

2. At the junction, take the road straight ahead signposted to Dover and Canterbury. Stay on this road until you reach the seafront.

3. Turn right along the seaside promenade (which later becomes a path running along the top of the beach) for 4.5km until you reach the Zetland Arms pub. Pick up directions for the main walk from **6**.

4. The short walk ends at the Zetland Arms, so just walk back along the promenade and before you reach Deal Pier turn left at the roundabout into Broad Street, which becomes Queen Street. Walk on the pavement on the right hand side.

5. When you come to the traffic lights at a five-way junction, walk around the corner into West Street and cross the road at the pedestrian crossing. Turn left and walk round the corner into Albion Place to reach the station.

6. For the main walk, walk in front of the Zetland Arms. Continue ahead along the shingle beach as directed by the signpost for the coast path.

7. When you near the road, come off the shingle and walk along this quiet lane in the same direction.

8. In about 500m the road bends sharply to the right to become Oldstairs Road. Here, take the footpath up the stairs to the top of the cliff.

9. You now walk along the coast path to Dover. The route is straightforward and well signposted, so details are only given for the trickier sections.

10. Follow the clifftop path for 2km, rising to a highpoint with an obelisk.

11. Shortly before the obelisk, take the left fork. As you continue, the old white coastguard's building will be to your right.

12. Continue on the clifftop for 700m and then make the steep descent to St Margaret's Bay. After the Leas you enter trees, eventually the path forks, take the left fork down steps to the bay.

13. Cross the car park and turn right along the seafront until you reach the Coastguard pub. Turn right alongside the pub garden and follow the road behind the pub.

14. Continue uphill until the road bends sharply to the right. Here, take the road straight ahead.

15. When this forks, take the left branch along Beach Road (which later becomes a car-wide gravel track).

16. In 400m you reach a junction with a two-armed footpath signpost on the right; here turn left along the wide gravel path (not up the steps ahead).

17. When the path turns to the right, go straight ahead up the steps onto Lighthouse Down and continue along the clifftop path.

18. In 700m, just before you come to a wood, turn right up the field, through the kissing gate and turn left on the chalk track signposted Saxon Shore Way.

19. In 400m, before you reach a road, turn half-left between hedges onto a path with a few steps to reach South Foreland Lighthouse. At the entrance turn left along a fenced-in path towards the sea and continue along the clifftop path.

20. You soon join a wide stone path, that descends from the lighthouse, laid by the National Trust to reduce erosion on this popular stretch. Follow this path for one and a half miles, it will take you around Fan Bay, over Corn Hill and around Langdon Hole.

21. On the other side of Langdon Hole, as the path rises steeply uphill with a handrail on the left, leave the stony path and turn left to walk along a wide flat shelf below the clifftop. Near the end of the shelf a National Trust sign To Visitor Centre, Dover Town and Port directs you up a chalk path that gently climbs the cliff.

22. At the top turn left to Dover Town and Port; you'll pass through two kissing gates. When you come to a concrete path turn left. Ignore turn-offs to the right. Eventually the path will take you under an A road.

23. The path soon becomes a road with a row of houses on the right. Continue ahead along the narrow East Cliff, then cross the A road and turn right along the seafront.

24. In 500m turn right between the two blocks of white Regency housing signposted England Coast Path. At your feet you'll notice the start of the North Downs Way.

25. Go straight ahead along New Bridge and down into the town centre underpass. Ignore turnings-off and continue ahead to Dover's centre along King Street. Ignore the sign to the visitor information centre and station, which directs you left.

26. Turn half-left across Market Square, along pedestrianised Cannon Street and continue ahead along Biggin Street. Then follow Priory Street round to the left towards the roundabout.

27. At the end of Priory Street, turn right to go round the corner to the pelican crossing and cross the road.

28. Turn left and walk to the roundabout. Take the first right into Folkestone Road. In 200m the road to the station forks to the right.

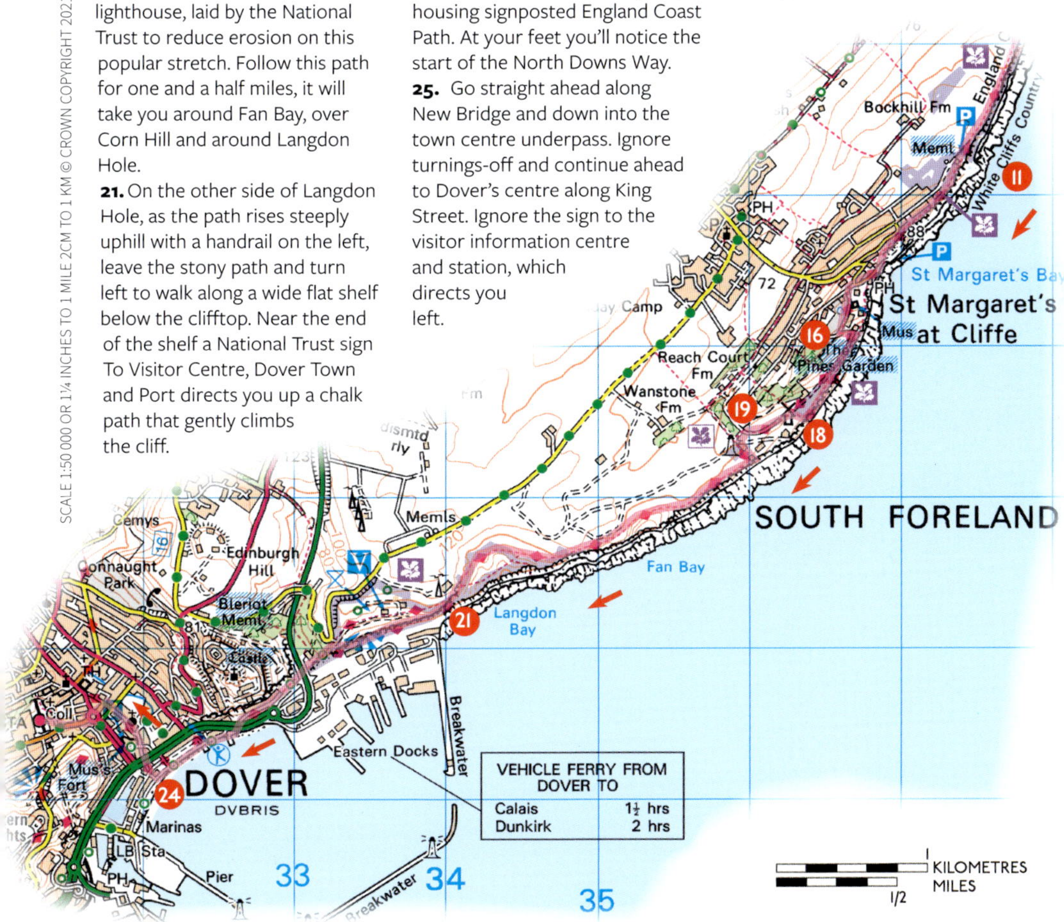

Featured summer walks

7 Manningtree Circular: damselflies & dragonflies
8 Winchelsea to Hastings: seaside & cliff walk
9 Otford Circular: summer meadows
10 Cuxton Circular: poppies & wildflower meadows
11 Folkestone Circular: seaside, art & fossils
12 Frinton-on-Sea to Walton-on-the-Naze: seaside & fossils
13 Shoreham to Eynsford: lavender fields
14 Lewes Circular: chalkland flowers

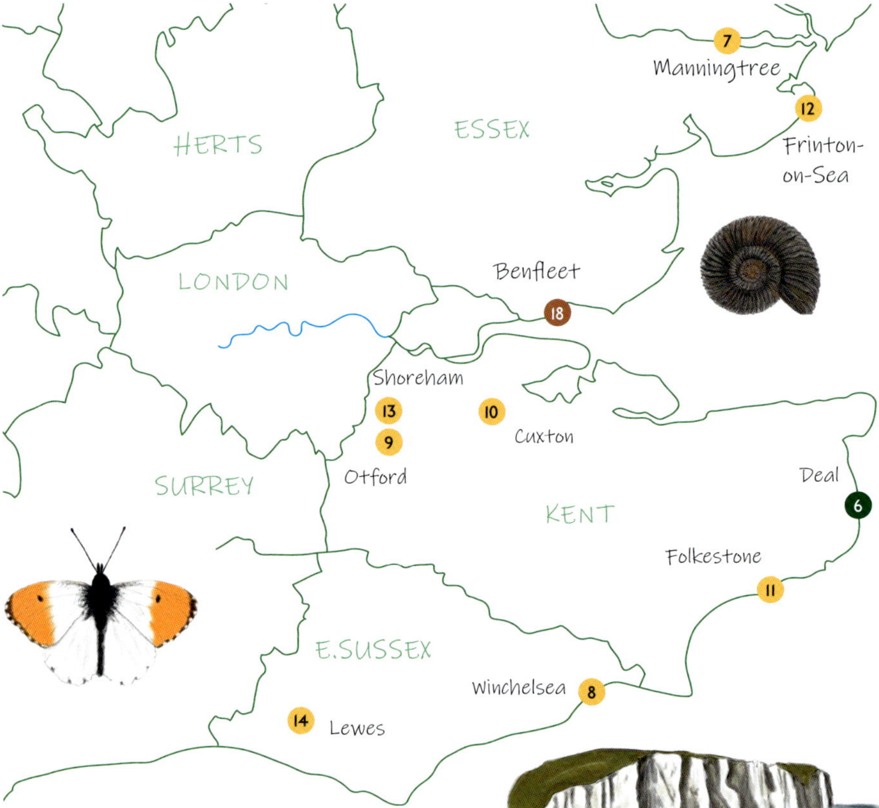

Other good summer walks

6 Deal to Dover: seaside & chalkland flowers
18 Benfleet to Southend: seaside

SUMMER

Summer invites walks along riverbanks, strolls through meadows and seaside expeditions, walks with pleasing places to stop along the way – to sit, to nap, to take it all in.

Long days encourage us to tackle something a bit more ambitious, so the longer walks appear in this section.

Summer is a good season to make up for childhoods undernourished by nature and missed opportunities to learn the names of butterflies, wildflowers and trees. A time to grab those pocket guidebooks bought with such good intentions or to fire up those underused apps.

As I've learned to identify a few flowers and butterflies, and then a few more, I've become more observant. The countryside has become richer and my enjoyment continues to deepen. Whole new worlds have opened up.

Forty years after the last world war, 97 percent of lowland meadows had disappeared. Their demise began with the ploughing up of meadows for arable crops in World War II, when more homegrown food was needed. Since then the expansion of arable farming and the use of chemicals have led to the disappearance of most of our chalk downland and wildflower meadows, and removed poppies and other wildflowers from our cornfields.

These phenomenal changes have gone almost unnoticed. Each generation tend to set their baseline according to what they experience in early life. For many people the current state of affairs is the new normal, the new baseline, against which they measure change. So I've determinedly sought out what was once abundant or commonplace but is now rare. Walks that demonstrate what my generation and those after me may have missed – a field of poppies, hay meadows alive with butterflies, downland carpeted with chalkland flowers.

By happenstance, an art theme also runs through this summer section – Constable country in the Dedham Vale; the bucolic landscape around Shoreham that inspired Samuel Palmer's etchings; contemporary art around Folkestone; and Lewes and Hastings, both popular places for artists, to live, work and exhibit.

Hot weather can make walking exhausting – unpleasant even. On these days I head for the seaside, to catch the breeze along the clifftops and to cool off in the sea. And what choice we have – hundreds of miles of coastline, edging Kent, Sussex and Essex, easily accessible from London, with some journeys under an hour. I enjoy these day trips even more now that I combine a visit to the seaside with a walk. Each of the three walks featured here begins or ends at a seaside resort and by chance each includes opportunities to beachcomb for fossils.

To top it all, among these walks you'll find summer culinary institutions: cream teas in cottage gardens, pubs beside rivers and fish and chips on the beach.

MANNINGTREE CIRCULAR, ESSEX AND SUFFOLK

A lazy summer stroll through Dedham Vale, the landscape of Constable's paintings.

INFORMATION

BEST TIME: First three weeks of June
LENGTH & DIFFICULTY: 8miles (13km); easy
APPROXIMATE TIME: 4hours
TRAINS: Liverpool Street to Manningtree (twice an hour; about 1 hour). Buy a day return to Manningtree
MAP: OS Explorer 1976 (Sudbury)
FOOD & DRINK: National Trust cafe at Flatford Mill and pubs and cafes in Dedham
PICNIC: Next to the river (no benches)
TOILETS: Manningtree station and Flatford Mill

In the 1970s this section of the Stour Valley was designated as an area of outstanding natural beauty, in part due to its artistic heritage. This is a walk to take your time over, a walk to be disrupted. To stop for a cream tea in the riverside cafe, to rent a boat and row along the Stour as it meanders through water meadows or to spread out a picnic rug on the riverbank, to lie back and listen to the wind shifting through the willows.

The day begins with a longish but decent enough walk to Flatford Mill, passing black poplars, Britain's rarest tree, which thrive in this waterlogged land. The place bristles with birdlife. But the walk you've come for begins at Flatford Mill. Here the River Stour first appears as two large ponds with an old brick mill and thatched granary sitting on the far side, once owned by Constable's father. Clumps of comfrey edge the ponds and white waterlilies sit on the surface. This is a popular place at the weekend.

Spend a few minutes here and you may spot the blue wings of banded demoiselles as their metallic blue bodies levitate above the water or glimpse the chasers, hawkers and darters of the dragonfly family.

Plummeting insect populations across Europe – one study revealed a 70 percent decline in a decade – has sparked a new appreciation of these ancient creatures. The brilliant website of the British Dragonfly Society helps you identify which of the 50 species you have seen. Around Flatford Mill there are blue-tailed damselflies, willow emerald dragonflies, southern hawkers, broad-bodied chasers, black-tailed skimmers and the red common and ruddy darters. The dragonfly's silvery net wings look pristine because their adult state typically lasts no more than two weeks in cold

weather and only up to six months in warm dry weather.

The lifespan of mayflies, another of the first insects on earth, is even shorter. The males spend their single day of life enticing females to mate. Look carefully and you may glimpse their translucent wings as they engage in their energetic dance above the water, a vestige of the thick clouds of mayflies that swarmed above our rivers until 50 years ago.

If there are few insects about or you'd like to see more, it's worth visiting the small RSPB wildlife garden over the bridge. The view immortalised in Constable's Hay Wain – the millpond in front of Willy Lott's house – can also be found on the other side of the bridge and is still recognisable after 200 years. A quick visit to the small free National Trust exhibition is recommended.

The walk continues through an open landscape of water meadows beside the sleepy River Stour, the boundary of Suffolk and Essex. So often rivers are hidden behind vegetation, but here meadows run uninterrupted right up to the water. There are endless places to sit and watch along these grassy banks. Occasional lines of grey poplars, willows and oaks provide shade. If you like wild swimming, the large millpond just before you enter Dedham is perhaps the best place for a dip.

The handsome village of Dedham and its commanding 15th century church were built with profits from the wool and cloth trade, industries that made this area one of the wealthiest in England. Pevsner wrote "there is nothing at Dedham to hurt the eye". The high street is a combination of medieval timber-framed buildings and grand Georgian residences – all very Jane Austen. Georgian frontages were added to several of the medieval buildings to modernise them, most easily seen at Sherman Hall opposite the church.

The route back is over gently undulating hills, through small woods and paddocks filled with buttercups. There is some road walking, but almost always along quiet country lanes. At the end, a footpath in the corner of an old churchyard deposits you back at the station.

DIRECTIONS

1. To exit Manningtree station descend the stairs from the platform and walk along the subway. Cross the space in front of the station on the first section of the zebra crossing and turn right down the slope to the large lower car park. At the bottom of the ramp turn left to reach a three armed footpath post.

2. Turn right and walk along a road for 600m. When it bends left, turn right onto a footpath that runs under a railway bridge. Continue on this path for about 1km. It will turn left and later right.

3. At a three-armed footpath post bear left following the sign to Flatford and Dedham. The slightly raised causeway follows the Stour River – initially hidden by reed beds. In 750m you pass through a kissing gate with a Dedham Vale National Trust sign; turn right here.

4. In 700m you come to a wooden bridge opposite a thatched cottage; on the way you pass a sluice and later Flatford Mill Lock.

5. If you want to visit the National Trust cafe, the free Constable exhibition or Flatford Mill (the scene of Constable's Hay Wain) walk over the bridge and turn right. If you'd like to visit the RSBP reserve or the loo, go over the bridge and turn left. Otherwise don't cross the bridge, go through the gates ahead and follow the river for just over 1km.

6. At the next bridge cross the river, signposted to St Edmund Way and Stour Valley path. On the other side turn left and continue along the river again for 1.2km, this time on the opposite bank.

7. Once you reach a road, cross and turn left. Walk over the first section of the bridge and turn right towards a gate.

8. Open the gate and follow the footpath. Just after the millpond, but before the white house, turn left through a gap in the hedge. Go over Dedham Lock, around the side of the mill and onwards until you reach a road, ignoring a left fork to a small car park on the way.

9. Turn right along the pavement and in 100m, just before the road bends to the left, cross the road and take the footpath on the left (initially a concrete drive). Cross the ford via a bridge on the right and then turn sharp right along a rather overgrown footpath, continue past a car park and then a pond on your right. Towards the end of the pond bear left, following the footpath and turn right along a drive that brings you to a road.

10. Turn right along the road and walk into the centre of Dedham and past St Mary's church. In 100m after the church turn left along School Lane and along the footpath at the end of the lane until you come to a footpath T-junction.

11. Turn left and walk halfway along the playing field (before you reach the cricket pavilion), turn right through a kissing gate. You now follow signposts for the Essex Way, with its poppy symbol, almost to the end of the walk.

12. Walk through several meadows and over a little wooden bridge then bear left diagonally across a field. Cross another small wooden bridge over a stream and go through a gate. Continue ahead along a wide grass path, with a hedge and then walls of outbuildings on your right.

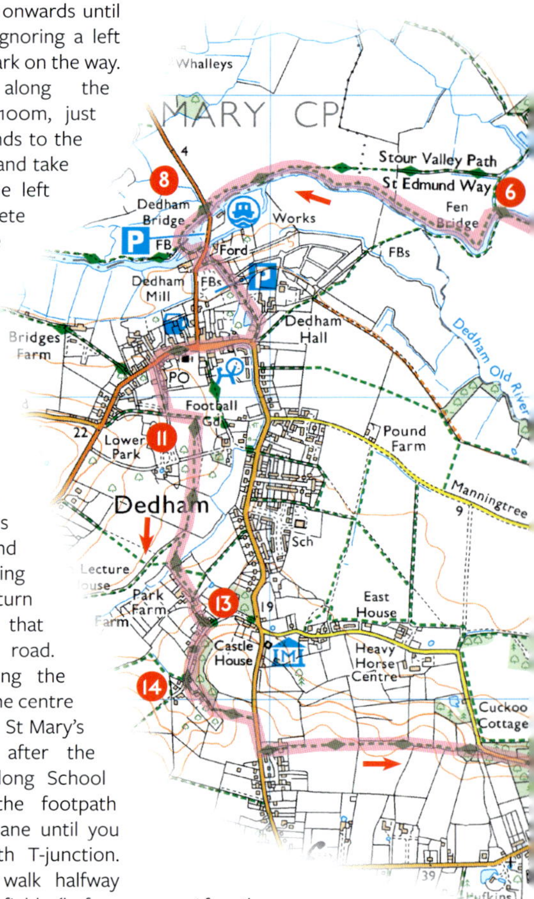

13. After the path bears to the right a bit, the footpath becomes a tarmac drive and leads to a road. Turn right and walk along the road for 200m (gently uphill and then down, past a number of typical Essex cottages).

14. At a three-armed footpath sign on the right, turn left along a gravel drive. When you reach a cottage turn left in front, then along its side. When you enter a meadow aim for the poplar trees on the far side and then turn right along the road.

15. In about 100m turn left down Anchor Lane. When the lane turns right, continue ahead on the grassy path and then between paddocks and through gates. In 700m you reach a road.

SCALE 1:25 000 OR 2½ INCHES TO 1 MILE 4CM TO 1 KM

200 400 600 800 1 KILOMETRES
200 400 600 1/2 MILES

16. Turn right along the road. In 300m, after the road bends to the right, turn left down a footpath. Follow the path half-right, diagonally across the field.

17. Cross the next road you come to and continue on the footpath slightly to the right, through paddocks and meadows, across a railway line and up into woods. In 400m at the top, just after a large Essex barn turn left along the gravel track.

18. In 200m at a grass triangle, continue ahead and then follow the track round to the left and continue until you reach a house.

19. After the gate turn right along the top of the meadow and follow the path until you come to a road.

20. Turn right along the road. In about 400m, just after the road bends to the right and after a red-topped post, turn left into a driveway and go past a big wooden gate. Near the end of the drive, turn right through a gap in the fence and follow the path along the edge of a field.

21. You leave the Essex Way after this field and walk into the churchyard. Keep to the left of the church and exit the churchyard in the far left-hand corner.

22. The long path eventually leads you to the station.

23. Turn right at the bottom onto a tarmac road and in 50m turn left along the footpath to reach the station.

Walk 8

WINCHELSEA TO HASTINGS, EAST SUSSEX

An exhilarating walk - perfect for a long summer day.

After an easy amble along unspoilt coastline, there's an up-and-down cliff walk with splendid views ending in the vibrant seaside town of Hastings. The day starts with a visit to sleepy Winchelsea, a major medieval port which, before the River Brede silted up, specialised in French wines.

I much prefer Winchelsea to neighbouring Rye. It has charm and antiquity without the crowds. Old characterful cottages line the streets, some half clad with overlapping clay tiles, others covered in white clapboard. More medieval and Tudor buildings and a 14th century church form a square around the graveyard in the centre of town, where swifts screech as they cut the air above. Visit in June and the handiwork of Winchelsea's invisible gardeners is in evidence. Immaculate roses hang around doorways and bloom on high brick walls, small roadside gardens burst with mounds of pink and blue geraniums, red valerian and cistus. The whole thing is almost a pastiche of an English village.

Winchelsea rises from flatlands, which you cross to reach the coast, reclaimed from the sea and grazed by sheep for centuries. Banks of nettles and reeds delineate the lines of sewers, Dimsdale, New House and Padium, local names for the ditches that drain this alluvial landscape.

The clean salt smell of the sea greets you as you climb the sea wall. The walk along the top of the pebble beach is particularly pleasant. Yellow-horned poppies rise from glaucous leaves among the line of wild plants running alongside the footpath. The jumbled colours of the pebbles are gorgeous: flinty blue, ochre, caramel, fawn, grey and bronze, with occasional flashes of white. This simple

INFORMATION

BEST TIME: First half of June (to see Winchelsea's roses at their best)

LENGTH & DIFFICULTY: 12 miles (19.5km); strenuous, several steep ups and downs

APPROXIMATE TIME: 6 hours

TRAINS: St Pancras to Winchelsea, one change (hourly; 1 hour 12 minutes, Sundays 1 hour 41 minutes). Return from Hastings to St Pancras with one change (hourly; 1½ hours), to Victoria (frequent, most with changes; around 2 hours) or direct to Charing Cross (twice an hour; 1 hour 35 minutes). Buy a day return to Winchelsea

MAP: OS Explorer 124 (Hastings)

FOOD & DRINK: Winchelsea Farm Kitchen cafe (closed Mondays) and plenty of choice in Hastings

PICNIC: Plenty of walls to sit on along Winchelsea beach and benches on the coastal path to Hastings

TOILETS: No toilet at Winchelsea station. Toilets after Winchelsea Graveyard, at Pett Level on the main road and Hastings

stretch allows plenty of time to gaze out to sea and in June feels very remote and wild. At high tide it's a good place to swim. Low tide reveals large expanses of sand and mud and sometimes you can spot the remains of a forest, not yet petrified after 6,000 years so still a bit squidgy. Walkers have scooped up hazelnuts along here, carbon dated to 5,200 BC.

The crumbly sandstone cliffs ahead are some of the oldest in the south-east. On the beach below and at Hastings, fossils of dinosaur bones and the footprints of iguanodon have been found, although you're more likely to find fossilised bivalves.

Up on the cliffs, landslips have swept away the coastal path, so a slightly boring detour winds through the sprawl of Cliff End and later Fairlight. When you return to the cliffs the sound of the sea accompanies you, seagulls cruise at your height and there are stretches with great views. On a good day you can see Dungeness and the White Cliffs of Dover in one direction, Beachy Head in the other and across to France.

As you near Hastings you plunge into the steep-sided valleys of Warren Glen, Fairlight Glen and Ecclesbourne Glen to enter ancient wooded gills – enchanted worlds delicately lit in green. Paths edged with small, crooked oaks lead down to a stream that trickles through a fetching mix of harts-tongue ferns, fronds of bracken and fountains of strappy sedge. Trails of ivy creep up trunks and hang down in clumps and everything is sprinkled with small pieces of sunlight falling through the canopy.

Shortly before you reach Hastings you walk across an expanse of closely cropped grass, where families picnic, children run and kites are flown. A sumptuous bird's-eye view of old and new Hastings can be enjoyed before you join the throng, a jigsaw of old tiled roofs, tall black huts used to store nets, fishing boats pulled up on the shore and the funfair and pier in the distance.

DIRECTIONS

1. Exit the platform, turn right across the railway tracks and walk along the road for 1km until it ends.

2. Turn right onto the main road and almost immediately turn right down a footpath, which eventually leads to a field. Turn left along the field edge. When the trees end, follow the path uphill.

3. Near the top of the hill, bear left to reach the fire beacon at the very top of the hill. Once you reach the top continue ahead, aiming for the field gate to the right of a black barn. Once through the gate walk along the road, cross the main road and continue on the road ahead, which is lined with flowers and cottages. When you reach the next crossroads turn right.

4. At the village square, go through the gate into the graveyard (halfway to the church, Spike Milligan's grave is on your right under an ash tree); 10m before the church, turn right to follow the path diagonally back across the graveyard and exit in the corner.

5. Cross a small road and then cross the main road. Turn left to walk along the main road for 400m. Follow the road as it bends to the right, then cross when you are opposite the tall, ruined wall. Climb over the unusual stile into the field.

6. Walk half-right, aiming for a gate in the fence, halfway along the field. Go through the gate and climb over the next stile on the other side of the footpath. Follow the footpath half-left across the field, aiming for a gap in the trees.

7. Go through a gate into the next field and turn left along the fence. At the end of the field, turn left through a gate and right along the road.

8. When the road bends to the right, turn left along a footpath that curves to the right. Follow the straight, rather indistinct, footpath as it veers away from the trees across the grazing marsh, to reach the sea wall in 1.2km. (In more detail – for the section across the grazing marsh – you soon pass over the Royal Military Canal, then aim for another bridge over a ditch. Aim for a further gate and then the path is pretty clear. Once near the road, climb over a stile on the right and through a kissing gate on the left.)

9. Cross the road and turn right to reach and climb the concrete path up the bank. Turn right along the shingle beach and walk for 3km, until you pass a caravan site at Cliff End (after passing a row of houses). Just after the caravan site, go up and down steps over the flood barrier, walk across an area of rough ground and turn right along a driveway.

10. Turn left along a main road. In 200m (after a white signpost pointing to Pett village) turn left up the second driveway. Almost immediately take the footpath on the right.

11. In 1.2km the path then bends right around the bottom of the field. In 20m take the left fork through a hedge (the cliff path has subsided, so there is now a detour around the large village of Fairlight).

12. You come out onto a road; turn right downhill and then follow the road as it bends left slightly uphill, passing houses on both sides. Take the first turning on your left, Cliff Way. Almost at the end turn right along a footpath between garden fences that soon becomes a gravel drive.

13. When the path ends, turn left along a road that becomes a gravel drive and follow this round to the right. Continue ahead until the road (which becomes Bramble Way) ends at a T-junction. At the T-junction turn left, walk to the end of this road and then turn right. The sea will be on your left and houses on your right.

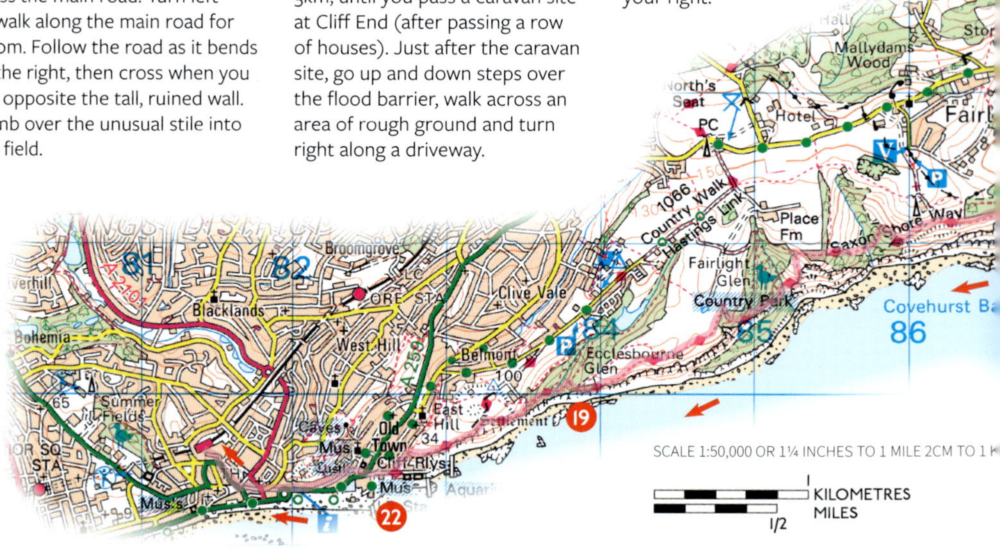

14. Near the end of the houses a footpath leads you into Hastings Country Park. Take the lower path over Firehills. Below the radar go through the kissing gate to continue along the coastal path.

15. You begin the descent to Warren Glen. When you come to a guidepost turn left down the stairs, signposted to Hastings.

16. After the steps ignore the path on the right and continue down into Warren Glen and up again, first on a path and then up steps, ignoring paths on the right.

17. The descent to Fairlight Glen soon begins. At post 17 turn left and at post 16 keep left. On the other side of Fairlight Glen, turn left at post 12. After post 8 keep to the left footpath.

18. The descent into Ecclestone Glen begins with a fenced-in meadow on the right. Towards the end of the fenced-in field, turn right and go through a gap in the hedge to continue.

19. The coast path from here has been reinstated after a landslide, so continue down and up Ecclestone Glen and along the coast path. You eventually come out into an open grassy area with Hastings ahead.

20. Follow the coast path close to the sea and aim for the tall fire beacon when it comes into view.

21. Descend stairs just to the left of the beacon, in the far corner. Turn left along Tackleway. At the end, turn right down Tamarisk Steps; halfway down turn left to Rock-a-Nore.

22. Turn right along the road. Ignore the first road off to the right. Cross the main road at the pelican crossing and go through the gap to the left of the Royal Standard pub and walk to the end of East Street. Turn right and then immediately left along pedestrianised George Street.

23. George Street will bring you out again to the main road. Continue along the main road in the same direction until you reach the roundabout. At the roundabout continue ahead along the pedestrianised road. Go down into the underpass and then walk straight ahead.

24. When you come to a junction of six roads, continue straight ahead, following the signpost to the station, along Havelock Road. When you reach the traffic lights cross the road and turn left up Station Approach.

Walk 9

OTFORD CIRCULAR, KENT

Pan out from your postcode on Google Maps and you'll see a large green protrusion nudging south-east London.

It's the tip of the Kent Downs. On a closer look, a chunk has been sectioned off by a lasso of motorways, but surprisingly you won't see motorways as you climb up and down this lovely section of the North Downs.

This summer walk is full of hay meadows, interspersed with ancient woodland, flower-filled downland and fine views. The meadows are in their prime from mid-June until the hay is cut from mid-July.

Since the 1930s we've lost 97 percent of our meadow grassland. Kent clings onto more than most and meadows still make up a fifth of its countryside. However, the majority are 'improved' – which means they've been ploughed, sown with productive but bullish rye grass and clover and laced with fertilisers, so sadly they are bereft of hundreds of species of flowers and grasses that thrive on unimproved soil.

But it's still a treat to see the improved hay meadows along this walk. The grass is high and soft sprays of Yorkshire fog grass add a purple tinge to the muted greens and browns. Dozens of brown butterflies fly haphazardly above the grass, occasionally joined by the orange brilliance of a fritillary as it speeds across the field.

Last year's beech mast crunches underfoot as you walk through mixed woodland. Red admirals rest in sunny patches, looking freshly minted in their bold orange, black and white, and very different from the painted ladies who've arrived from North Africa, whose colours appear washed out after their epic migration.

Somewhere along this walk, I like to lie down and look into the diorama of a hay meadow and breathe in its smell. A damp green lawn lies hidden at the bottom, out of which

INFORMATION

BEST TIME: Last half of June and first week of July

LENGTH & DIFFICULTY: Main walk 7½ miles (12km); shorter option ending at Shoreham 5½ miles (9km); moderate, a couple of steep climbs, steep descents and several stiles

APPROXIMATE TIME: Main walk 3¾ hours; shorter option 2¾ hours

TRAINS: Victoria to Otford (weekends hourly, weekdays twice an hour; from 36 minutes). Return from Otford (twice an hour; 41 minutes). Return from Shoreham direct to Blackfriars (twice an hour; 57 minutes) or to Victoria or London Bridge with change. Buy a day return to Otford

MAP: OS Explorer 147 (Sevenoaks)

FOOD & DRINK: Pubs and cafes in Otford and Shoreham

PICNIC: Benches early on

TOILETS: Otford station only

flowers rise to different levels. Low down are the golden clusters of bird's-foot trefoil: small, pea-like, delicate and puffy. Clover's pink and white heads are taller. Hawks-beard's dandelion-like heads, shiny buttercups and oxeye daisies reach for the higher levels. Meadow brown butterflies dip down into the long grass and somehow find space to weave through the multitude of stems; invisible obstacles send them back up only to dip down again. A grasshopper jumps into view and shifts up and down a blade of grass. Their collective hiss is still audible but not as loud as I remember from childhood.

The downland stretches are richer in flowers. A small detour leads you to a display of purple selfheal, interwoven with the yellow and orange of bird's-foot trefoil. From here there are extensive views across a valley of fields to the wooded Greensand Ridge. To the left, in the distance, the North Downs head off to Folkestone. Later, fat pyramidal orchids stand like lollies on downland banks alongside mauve scabious and the yellow spires of agrimony.

Poking up over the final downland ridge you can make out the Shard, the Gherkin and Canary Wharf. From the other side of the city – from Alexandra Palace or Parliament Hill – this ridge must be one of the faint purple hills that backdrop London.

On the way back you can stop off and explore the pretty village of Shoreham with its old pubs and catch the train back to London from there, or continue to Otford, to end at another attractive village.

DIRECTIONS

1. From platform 2, don't go up the stairs at the end. Instead about halfway along the platform, follow a Way Out sign up stairs and turn left onto a tarmac path.

2. Turn right along the main road and follow the path as it veers away from , but parallel to, the road. When you reach the road, Pilgrims Way East, turn right.

3. In 90m, at a two-armed footpath post, cross the road and walk up the first driveway signposted North Downs Way.

4. Climb uphill and then walk on the flat. After 700m you come to a kissing gate. Go through the gate and continue on the path ahead on the right-hand side of the meadow. At the end, go through the gate onto a road. Turn right and walk downhill on the road, signposted to Otford and Kemsing. In 100m turn left onto a footpath through woodland.

5. In 600m (ignoring turn-offs to the right and left on the way) you come to a very obvious footpath crossroads. Continue ahead, you pass a Kemsing Down information board.

6. In 50m the path will bend right, go downhill and then follow the path as it bends left.

7. When you come to a footpath T-junction, turn right and down steps towards a kissing gate (with a bench close by). Go through the gate and turn left along the hillside. Pass through a kissing gate (with another Kemsing Down information board) to enter another open area.

8. When the path forks, with a wooden footpath post in the middle, follow the left fork. In 100m go through a kissing gate and in front is a holloway; you'll be turning left uphill along the holloway. However it is worth taking this small detour: follow the path ahead, up through woodland to emerge onto flower-filled downland, with long views and benches - a perfect picnic spot. Return to the footpath crossroads and turn right up the holloway.

9. In 150m climb over a stile, crossing a couple of driveways beforehand. Follow the footpath sign ahead across the meadow. When you come to a line of large oaks, turn around and take the path that goes diagonally back across the field you have just crossed, aiming for the far-right corner.

10. Go through a gate and walk down a fenced-off section to the end and out through a kissing gate. Turn right along the drive and continue to the end. Go through a white gate and turn right along the road, which ends at a T-junction.

11. Turn left and in 75m, before a red post box, turn right along an easily missed footpath, initially with a garden fence on the left and then through a wood. Continue into a meadow and follow the path uphill and then over a stile in the corner of the field.

12. Follow the footpath on the left side of the meadow and then downhill aiming for a field gate at the bottom. Climb over a stile next to the gate and turn left along a road and in 20m turn right up steps and along a footpath initially between fences and continue ahead through two meadows. In the second field aim for the far right corner.

13. Climb over a stile to the left of a field gate and you are encircled by a fence with four field gates. Follow the blue arrow ahead and go through the gap to the right of the field gate towards a bridleway aiming for a white chimney. When you come to the house, turn left along the bridleway with garden fences on your right.

14. Follow the yellow footpath sign pointing ahead over a stile, cross a field, climb over another stile and soon go steeply downhill. At the bottom, go slightly to the right and then slightly left and walk along a path enclosed by saplings, then climb the hill.

15. Climb over a stile into woodland; the path bears left and then uphill. Come out onto scrubland and walk ahead, bear left through a gap in a line of trees and follow the path across the middle of the field, aiming for the fence and gate on the other side.

16. Continue on the farm track as it bends right downhill, then up and into a farmyard. Walk past the first two farm buildings and follow the farm track right, arriving at an information board. Follow the footpath sign left so the barn is immediately on your left and the round cattle shed on your right. At the end of the barn, continue ahead, as directed by a footpath sign on a wooden post, across the middle of a field.

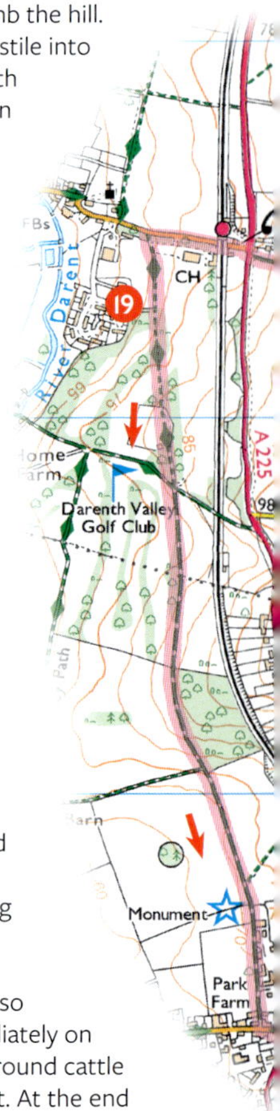

17. Enter the woods, follow the path ahead; eventually you cross a path and later descend a long flight of steps and continue along a lengthy flat section. When a fence comes into view on the right, a footpath joins from the left; continue downhill.

18. At the bottom, cross the A road and walk down the road signposted to Shoreham Village. If you want to end the walk here, Shoreham station is on the right before the railway bridge. Otherwise walk under the bridge and in 150m turn left along a footpath, having passed the entrance to Darenth Valley Golf.

19. Continue along this path between fences, with regular breaks for the golfers, for 1.5km, passing though the village recreation green with cricket pavilion on the way. You come to a quiet road; continue ahead for 700m until you come to Otford High Street. Cross the road and turn left along the road. Make your way around the right-hand side of the roundabout, aiming for the church.

20. Just before the church, follow the path into the churchyard (not to the palace). Continue past the church and into the graveyard with a high brick wall immediately on your left. Go through a wooden gate and along a tarmac path, which eventually leads you into the station car park.

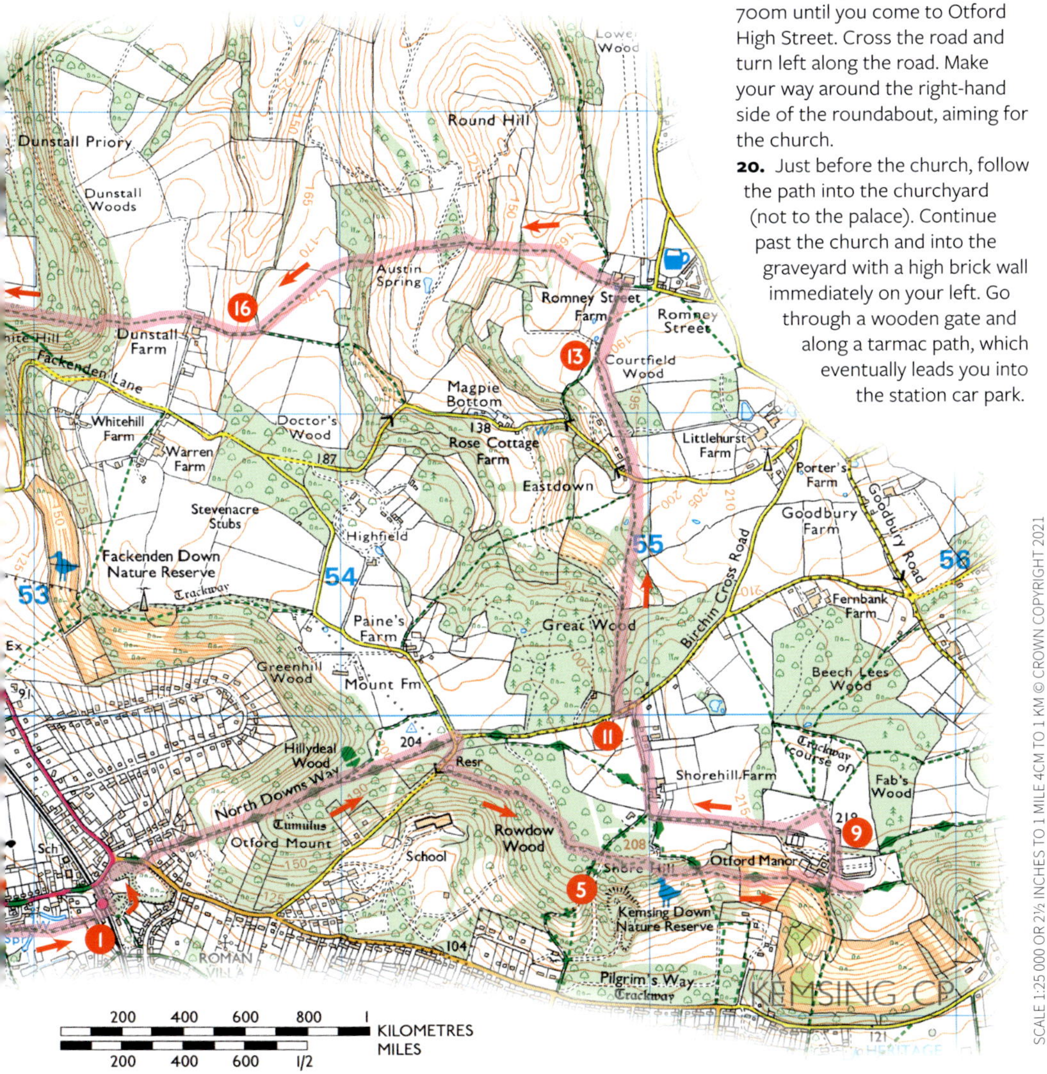

Walk 10

CUXTON CIRCULAR, KENT

In 2017, BBC news featured people flocking to a poppy field to take photos, highlighting how rare this sight has become.

Once poppies were so abundant in cornfields they were considered a weed; today they tend to only appear as an occasional clump at a field margin. The use of herbicides, more thuggish crop varieties, the change from spring to autumn crop planting and improved seed cleaning (which extracts the tiny poppy seeds from grain) are the causes of the decline.

The field of poppies on this walk was the first I'd seen. I have to admit my heart raced a little as I reached the middle. The banks of poppies conjured up the luminous red dots in a Monet painting.

While poppies won't disappear altogether, more than 500 wildflowers are considered rare or threatened in England. That's a third of our wildflowers. And on average one species of wildflower is lost from every county each year. Alongside this decline, a whole language is disappearing as common names such as eyebright, fat hen, kingcup, pheasant's-eye, venus's looking-glass, shepherd's-needle, lady's bedstraw, eggs and bacon and ragged robin no longer trip off children's tongues. At the same time, acorn, blackberry, buttercup and catkin have been removed from the Oxford Children's Dictionary, making way for broadband and cut and paste.

This shortish walk around Ranscombe Farm, nestled in the Kent Downs Area of Outstanding Natural Beauty, allows us to experience a lost world of meadows and arable fields alive with flowers.

The farm is the showcase reserve for Plantlife, a charity that seeks to protect and promote our wildflowers. The trip feels like a hike in the countryside rather than a walk around a reserve. Fields full of wildflowers are interspersed with ancient mixed woodland and there are views of the

INFORMATION

BEST TIME: Third and fourth weeks of June for poppies. Third week of June to the second week of July for fields of wildflowers

LENGTH & DIFFICULTY: 6 miles (9.5km); moderate, no stiles, several long gradual climbs, but plenty of benches

APPROXIMATE TIME: 3 hours

TRAINS: St Pancras to Cuxton, change at Strood (weekends hourly, weekdays twice an hour; 45 minutes, except Sundays when the journey out is 1¼ hours). Buy a day return to Cuxton

MAP: OS Explorer 148 (Maidstone)

FOOD & DRINK: The White Hart at Cuxton serves pub grub

PICNIC: Co-op on route for food, plenty of benches

TOILETS: None

hills and farms of the North Downs and the River Medway as it winds down its valley. The flowers of greater knapweed sprout from small artichoke-like buds in woodland clearings and marble white butterflies are drawn to the purple of their Catherine wheel flowers.

Old, solitary beech trees crop up among coppiced hazel and a line of grand oaks edge a wood full of coppiced chestnut, cut to their base to coax a clutch of new branches to shoot up, which in 15 or 20 years may be cut for fencing, roofing and flooring.

In June, the giant, dandelion-like seed heads of goat's-beard sit among the grass in Brockle's Field alongside oxeye daisies, yellow hawks-beard, purple pyramidal orchids, pea-like vetch, ugly common broomrape, wild marjoram and plenty of other wildflowers.

A bewildering array of white umbellifers flower throughout the summer, following on from cow parsley's May bloom. The ubiquitous wild carrot is my favourite, its flower a delicate snowflake made up of tiny blooms. Also known as Queen Ann's lace – due to a single red flower sometimes appearing in the middle of the lacy top, a drop of blood pricked from her finger. As the flower becomes a seed head, it curls itself into a claw and then a tight ball, making it easy to identify and a favourite of printmakers.

In other fields swathes of poppies erupt from an understory of daisies belonging to stinking chamomile. A few pink corncockles, once a common flower among arable crops, can usually be found in Kitchen Field, along the damper dip at the bottom. These geranium-like flowers on tall, slender stems are now classed as extinct.

In July the fields are sensational and full of butterflies. Poppies mix with swathes of vivid blue viper's bugloss, yellow St John's wort and the seedheads of opium poppies. Drifts of pale

yellow toadflax, our wild snapdragon, edge the field.

Only two percent of the meadows that were present in the 1930s survive today. This loss includes 7.5 million acres of wildflower meadows. Cornfields are no longer sprinkled with wildflowers and today's meadows and arable fields are what one report termed green concrete. But there's hope, as increasing numbers of farmers and landowners are showing an interest in reinstating wildflowers. There's now a National Meadows Day on the first Saturday in July, highlighting what we've lost and what we can reclaim. It takes 10 to 15 years to bring back a wildflower meadow, so hopefully our children and grandchildren will see less green concrete and many more wildflower meadows in their lifetime.

DIRECTIONS

1. Arriving on platform 2, cross the tracks either via the footbridge or level crossing. Walk along the road that soon bends left.

2. At the main road, turn right to cross the road at the pelican crossing. On the other side, turn right and then left along Bush Road.

3. Continue along this road for about 500m. Just after the Co-op on the left (easily missed as it's set back from the road), cross the road and turn right along Tar Tank Lane, a tarmac footpath.

4. Cross over the first road and continue on the footpath. Cross another road and walk up White Leaves Rise.

5. At the top of the road, go through a kissing gate, through a tunnel under the railway and into Ranscombe Farm Reserve. Follow the footpath that soon bends left.

6. In 400m (passing an information board on the way) you come to a footpath crossroads in the middle of a field, with a footpath post on the left. Turn left and walk up to the hedgerow.

7. Climb the stairs and at the brick railway bridge turn right along a footpath. The path soon forks; take the left fork.

8. Continue ahead on this path for 700m, through woodland interspersed with open glades, ignoring turn-offs until you reach a metal kissing gate.

9. Follow the path straight ahead, with a fence to the right, across Brockle's Field. When you almost reach the other side, the path forks; take the right fork to the edge of the field and go through a kissing gate into the woods (passing a bench covered in carved animals).

10. Follow the path for about 300m, to the very bottom of the hill, then take a sharp right, before a metal field gate on the right.

11. Ignore turn-offs to the left and right and continue uphill through the woods then downhill for around 600m. When you reach the bottom of the hill ignore a left turn and follow the path as it bends right. Ignore another left turn and when the path bends right continue ahead, and through gates into Kitchen Field. Turn right.

12. At a footpath crossroads turn left uphill. Pass a bench on the right and continue into the woods, ignore a right fork. Go through a kissing gate and turn right along the path, which keeps to the edge of the woodland.

13. In 800m you come to Birch Wood Corner (engraved on a wooden signpost on the left). Turn right along the farm track; you should have a hedge on your right and large field on your left. Follow the track as it bends right and continue downhill between two fields.

14. When you come to a field gate in front (and kissing gate on your right), turn left. Follow this track for 750m until it ends at a tarmac road.

15. Turn right along a gravel path, parallel with the road; when this ends continue in the same direction downhill on the road.

16. Take the first right along a wide gravel path (as a motorway bridge over the Medway comes into view on your left) into Longhoes Field. Follow this path along the top of the field (and then as it bears left) until you end up near the railway line.

17. In the corner of the field follow the footpath on the right and down steps into Pebble Lane. Turn right in the holloway and in a few metres turn left up a set of stairs.

18. Continue on the path uphill and then down and through a kissing gate and down a few steps when the path ends.

19. Now retrace your steps back to the station. Turn left through the tunnel and down White Leaves Rise. Cross the road and go down the tarmac footpath, cross another road and continue on a tarmac footpath.

20. Turn left along Bush Road until you come to the main road. Cross at the pelican crossing, turn right and then first left to reach the station.

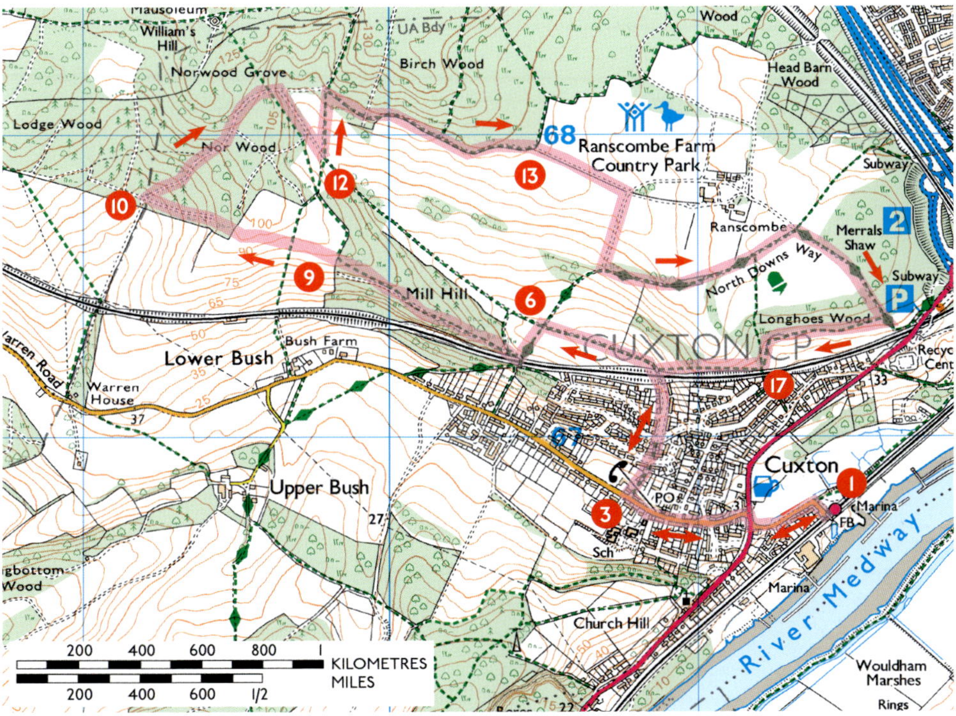

Walk 11

FOLKESTONE CIRCULAR, KENT

Unfashionable Folkestone is my favourite seaside town and this walk uncovers its treasures one by one.

After walking along the seafront the route leads you out into the countryside, along a wilder beach and culminates in a clifftop stroll with sea views across to France. And all this is under an hour from London.

Folkestone has been on the up for a while. The undercliff and beaches have been revamped, the quaint harbour area tastefully tarted up and there has been a concerted effort to regenerate through art.

The impressive Folkestone Triennial is held every three years in the summer and pieces from the town's growing public art collection crop up along the walk. Look out for: the Folkestone Mermaid by Cornelia Parker, pink houses in unexpected places, a huge upside down jelly mould and an enormous clifftop horn.

The day begins with a walk through Folkestone to the sea. As you near the front, the streets are filled with bright seaside light. The Leas along the clifftop, designed in the mid-1800s, has a wide strip of manicured lawn and promenade, an iron bandstand and neat flowerbeds full of slightly garish bedding plants, reminding me of childhood holidays spent along the south coast in the 1960s.

To reach the beach you descend the listed Zig Zag Path, with secret grottos and seats set in its artificial rock face. Blue and white pottery shards can be found in the Pulhamite, the cement made from waste material and used by unemployed men to build the path in the 1920s.

The award-winning Lower Leas Coastal Park fills the thin strip of landslip below. To the right a series of play areas hide among the trees. To the left a more formal section ends in contemporary flowerbeds. Three inviting pebble coves, ideal for swimming, lie in front of the coastal park.

INFORMATION

BEST TIME: June to August

LENGTH & DIFFICULTY: 9½ miles (15km); moderate, one strenuous climb with stairs and a couple of other steep ups and downs. Small boulders have to be crossed on one beach. No stiles

APPROXIMATE TIME: 4¾ hours

TRAINS: St Pancras to Folkestone Central (twice an hour, Sundays hourly; 1 hour), Charing Cross to Folkestone Central (hourly; 1 hour 39 minutes). Buy a day return to Folkestone Central

MAP: OS Explorer 138 (Dover)

FOOD & DRINK: Around 3km into the walk, lots of places to eat along the harbour arm. 7km into the walk the Cliff Top cafe, a basic place with good views

PICNIC: Plenty of benches, walls and grassy banks throughout the route

TOILETS: Folkestone station, Sunny Sands Beach and on the green on the return leg

A long boardwalk, made of railway sleepers, leads you across a wide shingle beach to the old harbour arm, now buzzing with bars and restaurants. The station, which once serviced Sealink ferries, has been brought back from dereliction and cleverly transformed into a public space. A footpath filled with wildflowers runs down the middle and leads you over the old railway viaduct with views of the quaint harbour below, still home to a fleet of small fishing boats.

Before leaving Folkestone, you walk around Sunny Sands, a large, flat expanse of bucket and spade beach, hidden at high tide. A climb up to the Martello Tower rewards with fine views of East Wear Bay and its long band of chalk cliffs, the North Downs falling into the sea. These forts were built in the 19th century along the south coast as a defence against Napoleonic invasion. Folkestone's best-kept secret are the ammonites, fossilised shark teeth, shells and belemnites found in the unspoilt cove below. The top finds are to be had around the headland at Copt Point, back towards Folkestone, but you can still discover fossils here among the rocks. Pick up the small black pieces of rock among the boulders and you are certain to find a fossilised shell and probably more.

The walk along the concrete sea defences of East Wear Bay is not the most beautiful, but it delivers a good dose of sea and feels remote. An unexpected, enchanting wood, lush with glossy hart's-tongue ferns and fairytale steps leads you to the clifftop and a cafe with views. Then it's along the clifftop with uninterrupted views across to France and back into Folkestone.

R488
HL 16

DIRECTIONS

1. Outside the station turn right and walk to the end of Station Road. Turn right, pass under a railway bridge and follow the road round. Cross over Kingsnorth Gardens and keep going.

2. At the roundabout keep walking and just after the roundabout turn left to cross the road (signposted to the Leas). Turn left and then right down Castle Hill Avenue. Make your way to the middle of the avenue and turn right along the tree-lined path.

3. In about 350m, when you reach a small roundabout, cross the road on the right to walk along Augusta Gardens. At the Kent Police building turn left along Trinity Gardens (still named Augusta Gardens on a street sign on the left). Cross Sandgate Road and continue straight ahead to the end of Clifton Road.

4. Cross the grass and turn left along the clifftop promenade. At the bandstand turn right and then left to descend the Zig Zag Path to the Lower Leas Coastal Park. At the bottom, continue ahead to the main path. Here you have two options.

5. To enjoy the flowerbeds, turn left and walk almost to the very end of the park, then turn right under an arched bridge and turn left along the seafront promenade. At the end continue along the path made from railway sleepers, across the shingle, in front of the flats.

6. Alternatively, to reach the shingle coves ideal for swimming, find one of several paths ahead leading to the promenade. As above, then turn left along the promenade and continue along the path across the shingle.

7. When the path forks, bear right to explore the harbour arm and walk to the end of the higher section. At the lighthouse, descend the steps and walk back along the lower section. For the shortcut, take the left fork and turn left along the renovated station platform and then over the railway viaduct, with harbours on your left and right.

8. Near the end of the viaduct, descend the steps on your left, walk ahead and turn right under the arches along Fish Market. Continue ahead until the harbour finishes and bear left to join the promenade circling Sunny Sands (the beach is covered at high tide). Walk around the beach almost to the end of the promenade and climb the stairs.

9. At the top, walk up the grass bank and turn right along the green next to the cliff.

10. When you come to the end of the grass continue along the tarmac path. Near the end of the path, at a metal post just after the first graffitied disused concrete building, turn left up a bank and then keep to the right of the golf course.

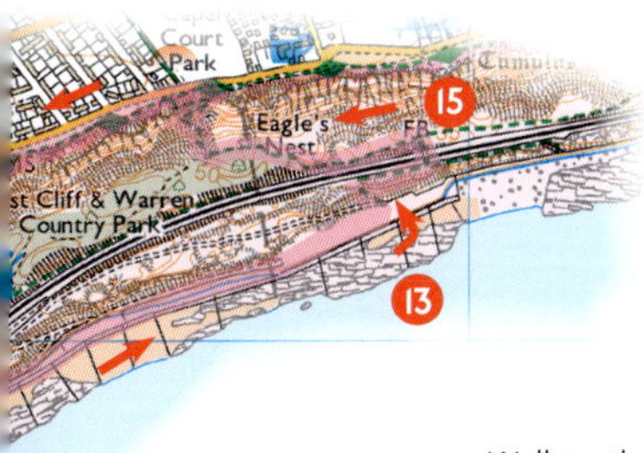

11. Walk to the right of the Lookout Station and down to the corner of the tennis courts. Cross a gravel track and take the footpath on the right, leaving the coastal path. When the path forks, take the right fork, which leads down to a small bay, where you can find black fossils among the rocks.

12. Turn left along the beach and at the end climb onto the concrete sea defence. Continue for about 1.2km along the concrete promenade. First the concrete is just a promenade, later it widens to the size of a football pitch. It then narrows again, this time with a lower level to the right. The path then dips and joins another football-pitch sized area.

13. About 100m from the end of this large area, turn left up a wide gravel track which almost doubles back, with a large square danger notice at the bottom.

14. After around 50m climb the stairs on the right up the bank. This path will take you to a footbridge over the railway. Once over, turn left along the path, which will eventually lead you into a wood. Well into the woods the path forks; take the right fork and continue along this footpath as it winds up to the clifftop.

15. After passing the cafe at the top, continue along the coastal footpath (in front of the car park). Later you pass a series of back gardens. When you come to a concrete drive, turn left and then right as you pick up the coastal path again.

16. After around 200m you come to a large grass area and the Battle of Britain memorial. Pick up the coastal path again on the other side. In another 400m at a three-way footpath marker and a Warren information board turn left downhill.

17. The path ends at a Martello Tower. Turn right along a road. Just after the wooden shed on the left, near the end of the road, turn left onto the green. Make your way across the green, aiming for the far left corner and walk up to the Martello Tower. From there retrace your steps to the station. (Alternatively, after the harbour, use a map app to walk to the station via the Old High Street, to savour Folkestone's Creative Quarter's shops, cafes and bars).

18. In more detail: drop down to the path and turn right. Walk along the green until you meet the steps, which take you down to Sunny Sands. Follow the promenade round to the harbour. Go under the arches, and up the stairs on the left, which take you up to the viaduct.

19. Pick up the path along the shingle by turning right off the station platform just after the toilets. At the end of the shingle, walk along the promenade. In the middle of the second cove, turn right up steps between beach huts. Turn left and aim for the path in front of the columns. After the columns turn right and follow the path until you reach Zig Zag Path, which you climb to reach the top.

20. At the top, this time turn right along the Leas and then first left along Clifton Gardens. After the first roundabout the road becomes Castle Hill Avenue. Continue ahead across two more roundabouts.

21. At the second follow Cheriton Road half-right ahead, and after you've passed under the railway arch, turn left up Station Approach Road.

FRINTON-ON-SEA TO WALTON-ON-THE-NAZE, ESSEX

This walk offers an interesting combination of Essex seaside resorts, followed by untouched wild coast.

The trip takes in two seaside towns, miles of superb beaches, crumbling cliffs dribbling out fossils and salt marsh cut through by wide creeks. It's a walk for those who want to explore a bit more of our coastline, enjoy being by the sea all day and like to people-watch.

The longer walk starts from posher Frinton-on-Sea. Bylaws, put in place a hundred years ago, were designed to create a more refined resort and dissuade 'the wrong sort'. As a result there's no pier, no pubs, no amusement arcades and no commerce on the seafront. Instead, a wide green swathe runs along a high bank and below, a utilitarian concrete promenade supports an endless line of multicoloured beach huts that disappear into the distance. In front, miles of flat, pristine sand is divided into rectangles by black breakwaters. There's so much beach that families can have one of these sections of sand to themselves.

Beach huts are painted in blue, green, brown or grey, selected from the colour palate in Tendering Council's Beach Hut Strategy; a few have names: Heaven Sent, Sea Breeze, Playtime, Life is a Beach. Pastel bunting is strung inside, mugs decorated with brightly coloured seaside scenes balance on windowsills. The smell of bacon wafts by. Silvered helium balloons in the shape of numbers sway in the large paneless windows. This is a place where families come to celebrate significant birthdays: one, 30, 50, 60. Outside, tables are laden with sausage rolls, plastic cartons of olives, crisps and cans of drink and three generations play frisbee and rounders on the sand below. The sand is exquisite. When dry, it coats wet feet like flour; when wet it's brilliant sandcastle material. A giant plastic ice cream cone welcomes you to Walton-on-the-Naze, quickly followed

INFORMATION

BEST TIME: June to August

LENGTH & DIFFICULTY: From Frinton-on-Sea 7½ miles (12km). From Walton-on-the-Naze 6 miles (9.5km); easy, flat apart from three flights of steps and no stiles

APPROXIMATE TIME: From Frinton-on-Sea 3¾ hours. From Walton-on-the-Naze 3 hours

TRAINS: Liverpool Street, change at Thorpe-le-Soken (hourly; about 1 hour 35 minutes). Buy a day return to Walton-on-the-Naze

MAP: OS Explorer 184 (Colchester)

FOOD & DRINK: Three cafes at the Naze Tower halfway into the walk. Fish and chips and more at Walton-on-the-Naze

PICNIC: Plenty of walls and benches throughout the walk

TOILETS: Frinton-on-Sea station, Frinton-on-Sea seafront and Walton-on-the-Naze seafront, and at the Naze Visitor Centre

by the blast of noise from the fairground on the pier (the beginning of the shorter walk). Here brightly coloured beach huts are stacked in terraces. Despite its popularity somehow Walton doesn't make too much of itself and has a rather unassuming, almost sad seafront, although I do like the corner cafe, popular with old bikers and their muscular machines. Perhaps recent efforts to regenerate will bring a bit more of the glamour befitting a town that welcomed steam ships from London in its Victorian heyday.

After a bit of a trek along the seafront out of Walton, the route runs along the edge of the Naze, a peninsula nudging into the North Sea, comprised of grass, coastal heath, scrub woodland and saltmarsh.

The Naze Tower marks the beginning of the peninsula. Built in 1721, it served as a marker for ships, guiding them into Harwich. The tower is now a visitor attraction, incorporating an art gallery, viewing platform and cafe. The modern Naze visitor centre close by offers information on local history, wildlife, geology, and walks (and has a cafe attached).

Coastal erosion claims an alarming one to two metres of land along the Naze each year. The medieval village of Walton now lies nine miles out to sea. Clifftop pillboxes from World War II have fallen onto the beach and the Naze Tower would have joined them in less than 50 years, without the recently constructed sea defences.

Try to reach the Naze as the tide recedes or at low tide, so you can walk along the beach and maybe dabble in a bit of fossil hunting. Few will realise the white shells with a slight orange tinge are fossils, exuded from the sandy red crag at the top of the cliffs. You can't miss these as you walk along the beach. Families sifting through shingle are after

shark teeth. The thin dark blades ending in a stubby root are so unblemished it's hard to believe they are 54 million years old.

Heavy black fossils capture bark, twigs and even poo, in unnervingly intricate detail. Over the last 50 million years they've been transformed into fossils made of iron-rich pyrite and are gradually being released from London clay.

The clay accumulated at the bottom of a shallow sea that covered this area of Britain, when the whole of what we now call England sat hundreds of miles to the south, where Spain sits today.

Low tide is the best time to find fossils, when they are washed into the dips and channels that form in the slippery beach of London clay. I have found fossils of fish vertebrae, squashed fruit, sharks' teeth and handfuls of the more common wood and poo fossils. Flints fashioned by our prehistoric ancestors have also caught my eye, but the bird skeletons and the huge megalodon teeth have so far eluded me.

As you wander up the unspoilt coastline of the Naze, wide views across Pennyhole Bay to the distant port of Felixstowe and up the Essex coast are welcome vistas after boxed-in London.

At the top of the peninsula the landscape flattens and runs into salt marsh. This is a good place to sit, to listen to the sea and to hear the calls of the oystercatchers and little terns and to watch turnstones busy themselves along the water's edge. You may even see a seal.

You can choose to walk along the sea wall to see the creeks and pools among the salt marsh of Hamford Water, before you walk back along the Naze through scrub woodland to the Naze Tower and retrace your steps to Walton.

This is a gentle, easy walk. A July or August visit allows full exposure to the seaside experience and the sea is a decent temperature for swimming. When I get off the train back at Liverpool Street station, I feel as if I've been on holiday.

DIRECTIONS

Shorter walk from Walton-on-the-Naze

1. Exit Walton-on-the-Naze station and turn right along the short station approach road.

2. When you meet the next road, keep on the pavement as it bends right. Cross over the next road towards the small green and turn right along the pavement.

3. At the end of railings, descend the stairs on the left down to the promenade. Turn left until you reach the pier and pick up the main walk directions from **8**.

Longer walk From Frinton-on-Sea

4. Once in the car park of Frinton station, turn left along a narrow road. At the end turn right, cross over Wittonwood Road and continue along the main road until you reach the sea.

5. Cross the green (keep to the right of the large toilet block) and descend the steps to the promenade in front of the beach huts.

6. Turn left and walk next to the sea for 5km until you reach the Naze Tower. In more detail;

7. Walk along the promenade in front of the beach huts for 3km until you reach the pier at Walton-on-the-Naze.

8. Immediately after the pier keep to the lower promenade, which eventually brings you up to the road.

9. For the next 1.5 km walk along the road next to the sea, first along the main road and then along East Terrace until it ends.

10. Continue along a tarmac footpath behind the beach huts, which runs into residential Cliff Parade.

11. Continue along the pavement and onto the grass. When Cliff Parade ends, continue on the grass. When the grass ends, pass to the left of a red brick shelter and pick up a footpath between the houses and the cliff, with a large anchor just to the right (ignore the slipway).

12. After the garden fences, descend the steps and continue at the same level on a wide grass path, which soon weaves between blackberry bushes. Stop when you come to a concrete path.

13. If you would like to visit the Naze Tower, toilets, cafes or visitor centre before going down to the beach turn left up the stairs.

14. Otherwise at the concrete path, turn right down the steps (ignore a turn-off to the right on the way down).

15. Before you reach the red lifebuoy holder at the edge of the sea wall, turn left along a path (with large boulders either side) down to the beach.

16. Walk along the beach for 1km – this is where you can find fossils. (If there's only 2½ hours before high tide – it's recommended you leave the beach two hours before high tide to be safe – you may want to explore the beach close to the path and then make your way up to the Naze Tower, walk along the green and then follow paths close to the sea and after around 1.5km you'll come to the sea wall. You can retrace your steps by picking up the directions at 18, except you would turn right along the sea wall).

17. In 1km, when you reach the top of the beach, the sea wall comes into view. Metal cages full of stones protect the big slabs of concrete that slope up to the sea wall. Continue along the beach and a large shallow pool appears on your left (in late summer this pool may have dried up exposing its flat base). At the end of the pool, a bank covered in brambles juts out a little. Continue on past an inlet to a raised causeway with a little tern information board on the top. Climb up the causeway and follow the path to the sea wall.

(You may want to turn right to wander along the sea wall for a while; if you do just return to this point.)

18. Turn left along the sea wall's tarmac path. When this comes to an end, follow the grass path down the bank.

19. The path soon forks; take the left fork. When the path veers right, continue ahead through an archway of shrubs and trees. Follow this path as it weaves through trees.

20. You will come to a clearing with a pillbox on the right, from here continue ahead, ignoring all turnings to the left and right. Then just aim for the Naze Tower which soon comes into view.

21. Retrace your route to Walton-on-the-Naze. In more detail;

22. Turn left after the cafe (to the left of the Tower) and descend the stairs. Halfway down to the beach, turn right along the grass path.

23. Cross a gravel track and continue ahead, up the stairs and along the path.

24. Walk on the grass and then along pavements next to the sea.

25. Once in the centre of Walton-on-the-Naze, drop down to the lower promenade and pass the pier entrance.

26. Continue walking along the promenade, past the first terrace of beach huts and right round the corner.

27. As you then bear to the left, turn right up a flight of steps with a handrail down the middle, between the beach huts.

28. At the top, turn right along the pavement. At the end of Southcliff keep on the pavement, passing a small green on your right.

29. At the end of Woodberry Way turn left to reach Walton-on-the-Naze station.

Stone Creek
Hamford Water
National Nature Reserve
Cormorant Creek
The Dardanelles
Standcreek Salts
Salt Fleet
Walton Channel
MHW
Hedge-end Island
The Twizzle
Landing Stages
Titchmarsh Marina
Walton Hall Marshes
Sewage Works
Creek Cottages
Walton Hall
The Naze Tower
PC
The Naze
Mud & Sand
Mean High Water
Mean Low Water
Breakwater
Mabel Greville Breakwater
Jubilee Beach
Groynes
Landing Place
Holiday Park
Sole Creek
Walton Mere (Boating Lake)
CH
Sch
East Terrace Breakwater
LEISURE POOL
WALTON-ON-THE-NAZE
Martello Tower
Coles Lane
Lane (Track)
Albion Breakwater
Marine Breakwater
Central Beach
LB Station
Pol Sta
B 1336
B 1034
New Walton Pier
Winchester Breakwater
18
17
13
1
27

SHOREHAM TO EYNSFORD, KENT

The sparkling River Darent runs along the bottom of an attractive valley, carved through the North Downs, on its way to the Thames.

INFORMATION

BEST TIME: First two weeks of July

LENGTH & DIFFICULTY: 5 miles (8km); easy – one option avoids the single climb (the shortcut is shaded blue on the map)

APPROXIMATE TIME: 2½ hours

TRAINS: Blackfriars direct to Shoreham (half-hourly; 1 hour), or Victoria to Shoreham with one change (half-hourly; from 45 minutes), or from London Bridge with one change (twice an hour; 49 minutes). Return from Eynsford to Blackfriars (half-hourly; 53 minutes) or with one change to Victoria or London Bridge (similar frequency and length). Buy a day return to Otford

MAPS: OS Explorer 147 (Sevenoaks) and OS Explorer 162 (Greenwich)

FOOD & DRINK: Pubs in Shoreham; Plough Inn, Eynsford. Drinks at Hop Farm Shop

PICNIC: Benches next to the river at Shoreham and Eynsford

TOILETS: None at the stations, but halfway at Lullingstone Country Park car park

Another greenbelt gem, protected thanks to that 1938 Act. This easy amble from Shoreham to Eynsford is a good summer walk. It's not too long, has shady stretches, is bookended by pubs in quaint villages and has grassy places to chill out by the river. But the main reason to visit in summer is lavender. It's claimed there's more of it in this valley than anywhere else in the UK. The walk takes you right into Castle Farm's lavender fields; the purple haze reaches its peak in the first two weeks of July and literally scents the air. The popular Hop Farm shop halfway along the walk sells dried lavender in bunches or little bags and garlands of dried hops harvested from the two hop fields you pass.

While the highlight is lavender, you can also see the white cross cut into the hillside above Shoreham commemorating those who died in World War I and visit Lullingstone Villa with its Roman mosaics and wall paintings.

Shoreham is where the 19th century artist Samuel Palmer produced some of his best work. He was one of the Ancients, a group influenced by William Blake and his romantic pastoral etchings and prints were inspired by this landscape. You pass Water House, where he lived, as you leave Shoreham.

The walk is mainly across farmland, but there are sections along the clear gentle River Darent. At the weekends there are classic summer scenes of children playing in the river at Shoreham and Eynsford and people sitting on the grass with beer in hand at Eynsford, with a backdrop of Tudor cottages and a 17th century bridge.

Towards the end of the walk you can choose to keep to the flat, although this means a 4km walk along the quiet

Lullingstone Lane. Alternatively take the rewarding road-free route up the North Downs, which will give you views back along the valley.

In the 1930s a site at the top of the hill was earmarked for London's airport. The war intervened, after which Heathrow was chosen. It is then down towards the high-arched brick viaduct and into Eynsford.

The only downside is the 1km walk along the busy main road through Eynsford to reach the station.

DIRECTIONS

1. The route is pretty self-evident, so I haven't mentioned every stile and gate.

2. Exit platform 2, go past the stairs to the footbridge, turn right before the car park and descend the stairs to the road.

3. Turn right along the road. Shortly after the railway bridge, follow the permissive footpath on the right, parallel to the road.

4. At the end of the field, follow the path right. You soon reach a flint wall, turn left through the gate with a Commonwealth War Graves sign nearby, into the churchyard, walk between yew trees and exit the other side.

5. Continue ahead, past the Samuel Palmer pub, and follow the road until it reaches the bridge over the River Darent. Don't cross the bridge. Instead keep straight ahead, passing the war memorial on your left and follow the path along the course of the river.

6. In 500m follow the path left over a bridge and round to the right between garden fences. Follow the tarmac road as it bends to the left. Just before the road goes uphill take the footpath on the right, next to the river.

7. Follow the path along the course of the river for 500m, then through fields for 800m (first aiming for a line of poplars and then onwards across more fields) until you come to a road. Cross the road and climb up a few steps, following the permissive path sign. You pass fields of lavender and hops before the path ends at a road.

8. Turn left into Lullingstone Country Park. Before the car park turn right to walk in front of the visitor centre. Continue on between the outside tables, past the Acorn Adventure playground and just before the field turn right and then left to follow the river.

9. In 500m you emerge into what looks like a small car park. Exit to the right of a green car barrier and turn left along the drive, passing Lullingstone Castle on your right. The path becomes a quiet road.

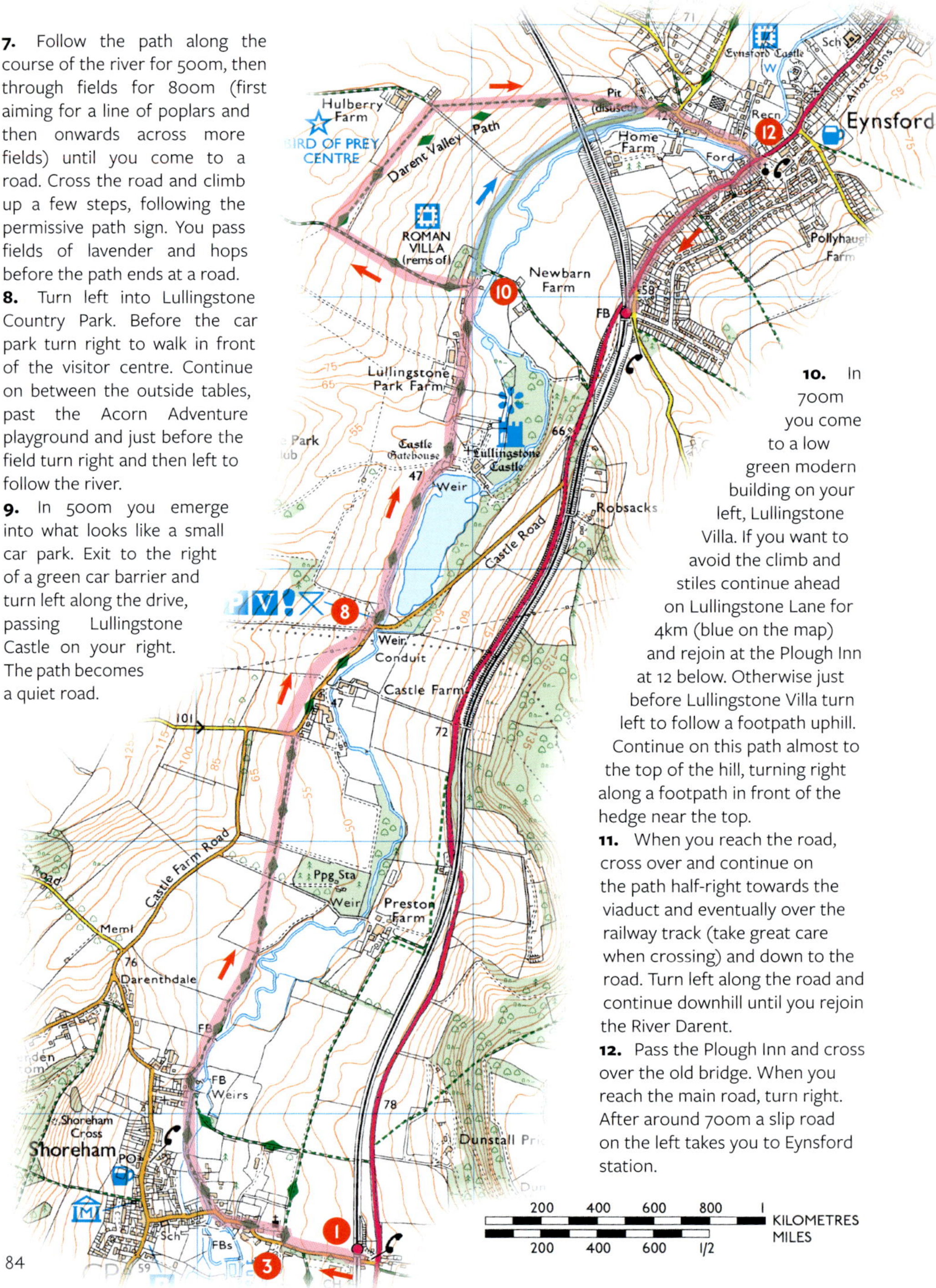

10. In 700m you come to a low green modern building on your left, Lullingstone Villa. If you want to avoid the climb and stiles continue ahead on Lullingstone Lane for 4km (blue on the map) and rejoin at the Plough Inn at 12 below. Otherwise just before Lullingstone Villa turn left to follow a footpath uphill. Continue on this path almost to the top of the hill, turning right along a footpath in front of the hedge near the top.

11. When you reach the road, cross over and continue on the path half-right towards the viaduct and eventually over the railway track (take great care when crossing) and down to the road. Turn left along the road and continue downhill until you rejoin the River Darent.

12. Pass the Plough Inn and cross over the old bridge. When you reach the main road, turn right. After around 700m a slip road on the left takes you to Eynsford station.

Walk 14

LEWES CIRCULAR, EAST SUSSEX

An amphitheatre of hills surrounds the flood plain of the River Ouse and the historic town of Lewes.

These downland hills are bare and whale-like and this walk runs along the tops, dipping twice into valleys that allow rail and roads into the enclosed plain. Part of the South Downs, our most recently designated National Park, these hills are the closest we get to dales or mountains near London.

If you can resist the cafes and antique shops of Lewes, 15 minutes after leaving the station you suddenly enter the sparse landscape of these ancient chalk domes, gently sloping into dry valleys with the circle of a dew pond sitting at the bottom. There are no cars, no roads, no houses.

In June, skylark after skylark rise and sing. Clusters of yellow horseshoe vetch, purple pyramidal orchids and bird's-foot trefoil flower in the short grassland, accompanied by blue butterflies and the burnet moth with its flashy red on black. You're entering the world of rare chalk grassland. England has lost 80 percent of its chalk downland since the 1940s. Despite this, 50 percent of the world's surviving chalk grassland is found in the UK and much of this is concentrated in southern England.

This habitat hasn't occurred naturally but is the product of human activity. Chalk hills were first deforested, then subject to low-level grazing by sheep or cows. The grazing prevents shrubs from taking hold and keeps grass short, which together with the thin, nutrient-poor soil prevents any one plant from dominating. The result, up to 45 different flowers, herbs and other plants, can be found in one square metre. These in turn support a diverse range of butterflies and other insects.

In August, flowers rise to knee height along the hillside of Southerham Farm Nature Reserve. The reddish purple of

INFORMATION

BEST TIME: August
LENGTH & DIFFICULTY: Main walk: 15½ miles (25km); strenuous. Shorter option: ending at Southease 8½ miles (14km); strenuous. Shortest option: ending at Glynde 4 miles (6.5km); moderate. You have to cross the A27 (a dual carriageway) on the main walk and the walk ending at Southease
APPROXIMATE TIME: Main walk 7¾ hours. Ending at Southease 4¼ hours. Ending at Glynde 2 hours
TRAINS: Victoria to Lewes (twice an hour, hourly on Sundays; from 1 hour 2 minutes). For the shorter walks buy a day return from London to the station you plan to walk to (Glynde or Southease)
MAP: OS Explorer OL 11 (Brighton)
FOOD & DRINK: Places to eat in Lewes, Little Cottage Tea Rooms in Glynde (Thursday to Sunday 11am or 11:30am to 4pm). Courtyard cafe at Southease open until 4pm
PICNIC: On top of the hills, although there are no benches
TOILETS: Lewes station and just before Glynde station

wild marjoram dominates, interwoven with white umbels of wild carrot, the purples of thistle and knapweed and yellows of ragwort and feverfew.

With luck, somewhere along the walk you'll spot the exquisite blue of round-headed rampion with its sea anemone flower heads, nicknamed the Pride of Sussex.

When you reach the ridge there are fantastic views across the Weald to the North Downs and Greensand Ridge – the hills that hold the orchards you may visit in autumn.

You descend to the small village of Glynde where you can stop for tea and cake in the garden of a typical Kentish cottage, with its small-paned windows and steep roof of weathered clay tiles. You can choose to catch the train back to Lewes from the village or continue on.

The longer options require some walking along quiet roads, climbs that get your heart pumping and there's a bit of a slow trudge uphill on the longest walk. The rewards are long ridge walks, views of the south coast to the Seven Sisters chalk cliffs and a sense of achievement as you look back and trace your route over the hills on the other side of the plain.

And when you're out all day, the evening light – quite magical on this landscape – compensates for the hazy daytime views so common at this time of year.

DIRECTIONS

Section one: Lewes to Glynde

1. Climb the stairs and go along the walkway to the station's main exit.

2. Once out of the station turn right along the road. When you come to a road junction turn right down Lansdown Place.

3. Continue ahead at a mini roundabout. Later at traffic lights turn right along High Street (initially pedestrianised); in 400m it ends at a main road. Cross the main road and walk up narrow Chapel Hill opposite.

4. The road climbs for 600m, ending at Lewes Golf Club.

5. At the end of the first golf club car park turn right along the footpath, go through the gate and follow the main track.

6. In 450m the path forks. Take the left fork to carry on uphill.

7. Continue on this path until you go through a metal gate at the top of the ridge (passing through a gate on the way).

8. In about 30m at a footpath crossroads, turn right along a path that leads gently uphill.

9. Climb over the small summit and then follow the path downwards.

10. When you come to a chalky footpath crossroads (in a dip, with a small wood on your left) go straight ahead uphill again, aiming for a field gate and steps.

11. Once over the steps, continue for almost 1km.

12. At a footpath crossroads, with a gate and steps on your right (and 200m before you reach a fence and gate), take the easily missed faint grass path on your left over the brow of the hill and then down.

13. At the trees, go through a gate and down through fields to Glynde. Turn left along the road (Glynde Tea Room is almost in front of you).

14. Turn right along the main Glynde road. In about 350m you come to Glynde station.

Section two: Glynde to Southease

15. Continue to follow the main road as it winds through Glynde. In 700m cross the very busy A27.

16. Continue ahead along a quiet road, which later becomes a gravel track. After around 2.5km you reach the top of the ridge with views of the sea.

17. At the footpath crossroads, turn right to follow the South Downs Way (SDW).

18. You keep on this national trail for the next 10km until you turn off to Lewes. In more detail;

19. Walk along the ridge and gently down. Follow the path as it bears round to the left.

20. In 100m, before a fence on the left, take the thin path down towards the bridge over the main road.

21. Go through a gate and down a wide chalk path towards the main road. When the footpath forks take the left fork over the bridge signposted SDW.

22. On the other side of the bridge, follow the winding road for 400m, until you reach Southease station.

Section three: Southease to Lewes

23. Go through the level crossing and along a quiet road for 1km until you reach a main road. On the way you pass a small green and medieval church on your left.

24. Turn right along the main road and then cross this busy road to reach Gorham's Lane. Then immediately cross Gorham's Lane and go through a gate into a field signposted SDW.

25. The path winds down to the bottom of the valley where you reach a T-junction; turn left along a farm track. After around 1.2km next to an area with farm machinery, take the footpath on the right signposted SDW.

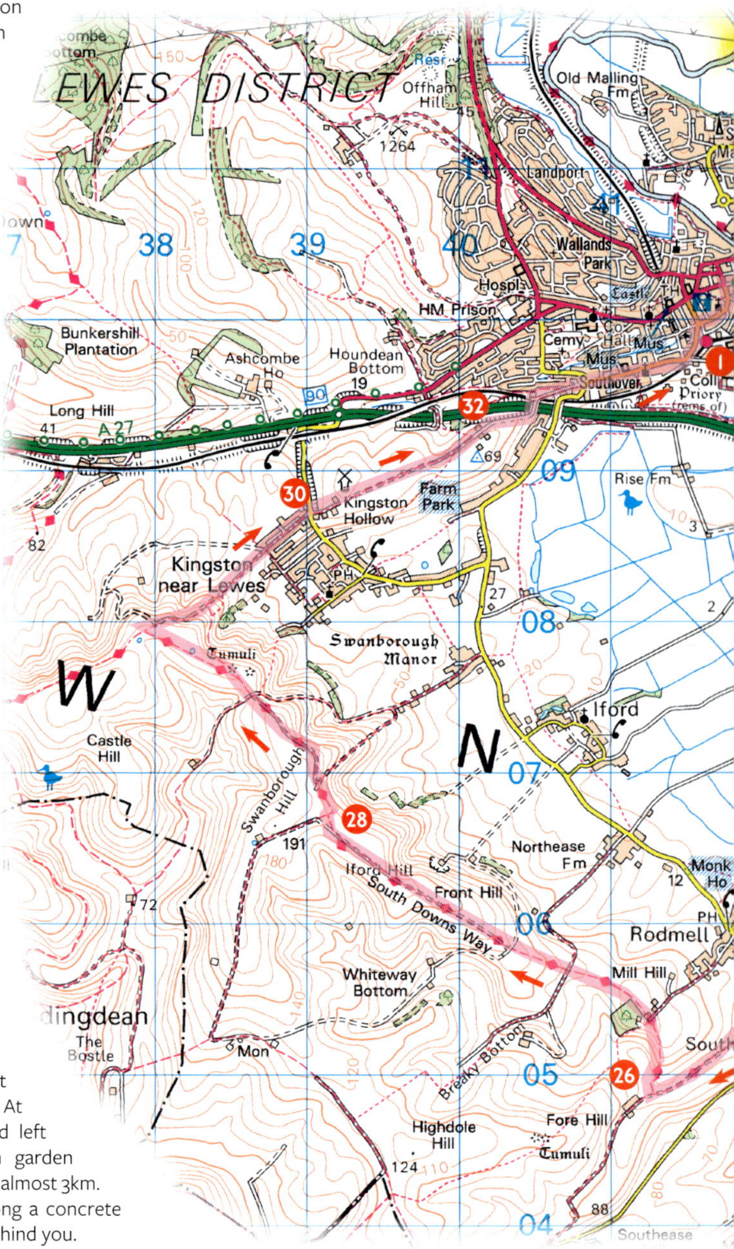

26. Then in 100m turn right through a gate and walk uphill. At the top go through a gate and left along a path initially between garden fences. Continue on this path for almost 3km. Much of the later section is along a concrete farm track; the best views are behind you.

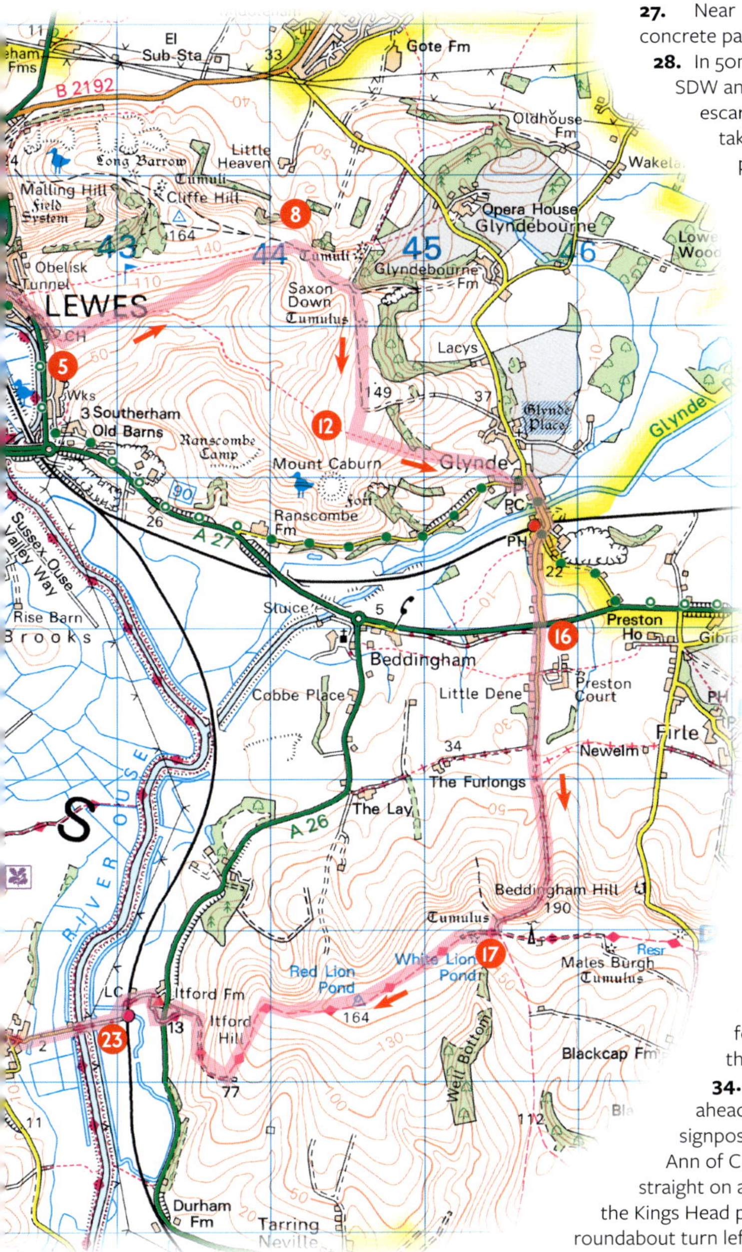

LE 1:50 000 OR 1¼ INCHES TO 1 MILE 2CM TO 1 KM © CROWN COPYRIGHT 2021

27. Near the top of the hill when the concrete path turns to the left, go right.

28. In 50m turn left to follow the SDW and walk along the top of an escarpment for 1.2km. Before you take the turn-off to Lewes, the path dips and you come to a footpath crossroads with a cattle grid on the left. Continue straight on for another 200m and at the three-armed footpath sign, turn right along the bridleway signposted to Kingston and Lewes.

29. Descend the ridge and continue along the chalk path, which eventually becomes a road with houses either side and later ends at a main road.

30. Cross the main road to walk up Juggs Road, which fairly soon becomes a grassy path across fields.

31. At the end of open fields, take the path ahead, but slightly to the left, between trees and hedges.

32. This path eventually runs into a tarmac lane and takes you into Lewes (after crossing a bridge over the A27) and ends as a short residential street.

33. When you come to a main road, turn left. Continue for 700m until the turn-off for the station.

34. In more detail, go straight ahead at the mini roundabout signposted to Town Centre, past Ann of Cleaves house on your left and straight on at the mini roundabout with the Kings Head pub on your left. At the next roundabout turn left along Station Road.

1 KILOMETRES
MILES 1/2

Featured autumn walks

15 East Farleigh to Yalding: apple orchards
16 Richmond Circular: deer rut
17 Sevenoaks Circular: sweet chestnuts & deer rut
18 Benfleet to Southend: brent geese
19 Wendover to Princes Risborough: autumn leaves
20 Guildford to Chilworth: autumn leaves

Other good autumn walks

3 Tring Circular: autumn colour
4 Chartham to Canterbury: apple orchards
9 Otford Circular: autumn colour
26 Box Hill Circular: autumn colour

AUTUMN

Summer usually slips into September, bringing warmth to days still long enough for the seaside walks in the summer section. But by late November it already feels like winter. Trees are bare, the sky is grey and the days are short.

Like spring, autumn presides over tremendous change. But when does autumn start? One method selects 1 September, another the autumnal equinox in late September. I've chosen the beginning of September, so the autumn section encapsulates apple orchards at their peak. My concept of autumn couldn't countenance ripe apples – that archetypal symbol of autumn – being shunted back into summer. It's a reminder, perhaps, that our seasons are social constructs. In the medieval period, 'Somer' began in February and ended in July, and it wasn't until the 1500s that spring was used to denote a separate season. Instead of seasons, months were codified, each associated with particular events or tasks – 'labours of the months'. June was when thistles and other weeds were pulled from crops, September was the time for threshing, and in October corn was ground. There was, however, a period between summer and winter called harvest, which in the 17th century became fall and in the 18th century began to be described as autumn.

Like spring, autumn is a season ideal for walking: it's not too hot and has a particular beauty. As the earth turns on its axis, the sun slants in at an angle, suffusing everything with a golden glow. Rain encourages fungi to emerge through leaf mould and mushrooms form rings in meadows.

The series of natural events that unfold throughout autumn are worth seeking out and are easily accessed from London: Kent orchards loaded with fruit, Thames Estuary mudflats alive with migratory birds, the autumn colours of Chiltern beechwoods and rutting deer in royal parks. In September you can return from most walks with a haul of sloes for sloe gin and in October you'll find sweet chestnuts to roast in the oven.

As you strike out, notice the influx of birds. Migrants from Europe, Russia, Scandinavia and Iceland swell resident populations of chaffinches, goldcrests, long-tailed (and other) tits and contribute new additions such as bramblings. From October, winter thrushes, fieldfares and redwings enter Britain in search of milder weather and berries.

The timing and intensity of autumn colour can vary. In some years trees hold on to their leaves for weeks, especially if frosts come late and the weather is dry. In other years high winds, hard frosts or stormy weather can bring the show to a sudden end. The Forestry Commission website identifies the best time to see autumn colour each year.

Autumn events are short-lived and easily missed. Apples are picked by mid-September and trees may only blaze yellow, amber and red for a fortnight. So, like spring, it's worth earmarking a few days at the right time.

EAST FARLEIGH TO YALDING, KENT

Tiny green trees, printed in neat diagonal lines, represent orchards on Ordnance Survey maps.

As you hike through Kent, follow your route on a map and you'll notice many of these fields are no longer orchards. As on this walk, trees have been grubbed up and replaced with crops or pasture. But thankfully there are still plenty of orchards to enjoy on this exploration of the fruit farms surrounding Maidstone and along the southern slopes of the Greensand Ridge.

These are not the orchards of children's picture books with their gnarled tree trunks and floppy canopies dotted with fruit; they're commercial orchards with young spindly trees laid out in regimented lines. In September you'll enjoy scenes of extravagant abundance: endless trees crammed with clusters of swollen red apples. They'll be at their peak in the first two weeks of September.

This walk takes you right into the orchards, field upon field of fruit trees. Plywood packing crates tower high at the side and are placed at regular intervals next to the rows of trees ready for the pickers. Large collecting bags are strapped tightly to the fronts of the workers, some of whom have harvested here for decades, and apple trains move lines of huge crates brimming with fruit.

The high hedges shielding the orchards are decorated with bunches of tiny red haws, firm glossy rosehips and ivy flowers that provide late nectar for the bees' and butterflies' last hurrah. Each seed head of old man's beard is a firework of silver spray, and the blackberries – often so bitter in August – now have that sweet taste remembered from childhood.

Damsons were a popular hedging tree in Kent and squashed purple fruit at your feet alert you to a potential haul. By early September damsons are going over, but you should find enough fruit to make a crumble, a pot of jam or

INFORMATION

BEST TIME: First two weeks of September

LENGTH & DIFFICULTY: 12 miles (19km); easy

APPROXIMATE TIME: 6 hours

TRAINS: All outbound journeys require one change. Charing Cross to East Farleigh (twice an hour, Sundays hourly; 1 hour 15 minutes). From St Pancras, to East Farleigh (hourly; from 1 hour 13 minutes). Return from Yalding to Charing Cross, change at Tonbridge (twice an hour, Sunday hourly; 1 hour 12 minutes) or to St Pancras, two changes (twice an hour; from 1 hour 23 minutes). Buy a day return to Yalding

MAP: OS Explorer 148 (Maidstone)

FOOD & DRINK: Pub grub at Bull Inn at Linton, halfway through the walk or earlier at Chequers Inn at Loose

PICNIC: Bench further uphill from Chequers Inn overlooking Loose mill pond or along the Greensand Way somewhere after Linton but very few benches

TOILETS: No toilets at the stations or along the walk

damson gin. I love their tart taste and so once a year I'm prepared to stand over the stove, fishing out stones as the flesh loosens.

Kent history is written all over this little-changed landscape. As you begin the walk, you cross East Farleigh Bridge, possibly one of the finest medieval bridges in the south of England. Along the way you pass half-timbered houses, a traditional barn at Buston Manor and walls made of Kentish ragstone, possibly sourced from the now-defunct West Farleigh quarry. The white cowls and upside-down cones of oast houses seem to appear in every vista. While most are now converted into homes, these old hop-drying kilns are a reminder that the orchards were probably once filled with hops. In September up to 200,000 people would come into the county to help with the harvest. Whole East End families would return to the same hop farm each year, arriving on trains from London Bridge called hoppers specials, exchanging the grime of London for a few weeks in the country.

Before you enter into the heart of the orchards you follow the course of the River Loose, once cluttered with mills built to provide energy for the fulling (cloth thickening and cleaning) and paper-making industries, for which the area was famous. Once in Loose, you walk along a narrow causeway running down the middle of the village mill pond. The sound of running water accompanies you around the village, spilling from spouts into the mill pond and coursing along channels beside the road.

Halfway through the walk, it's worth savouring the view across the Weald from the terrace of the Bull Inn. On a clear day, you can make out the distant South Downs. The prettiest orchards are laid out on the slopes below and along the Greensand Ridge ahead. You are likely to disturb green woodpeckers probing for ants in the strips of grass between the fruit trees and hear buzzards mew as they circle above. The route takes you through woods of coppiced sycamore, which once supplied stakes for the hop fields and orchards.

The only downside to this walk is the initial mile and a half walking along country roads with some traffic. The route through Yalding to the station is also quite traffic-heavy, although Yalding's old buildings, long stone medieval bridge and canalside make it more bearable.

DIRECTIONS

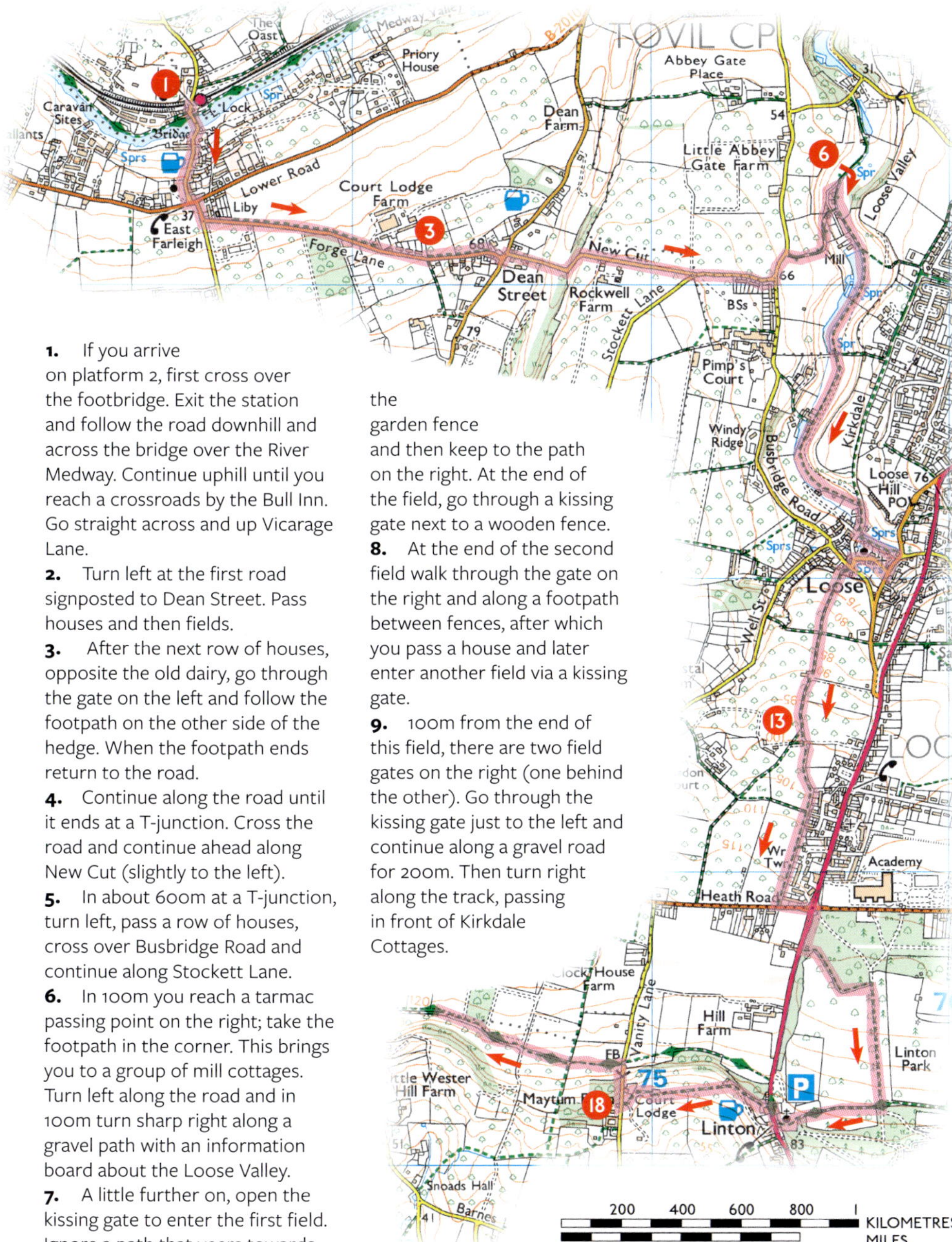

1. If you arrive on platform 2, first cross over the footbridge. Exit the station and follow the road downhill and across the bridge over the River Medway. Continue uphill until you reach a crossroads by the Bull Inn. Go straight across and up Vicarage Lane.

2. Turn left at the first road signposted to Dean Street. Pass houses and then fields.

3. After the next row of houses, opposite the old dairy, go through the gate on the left and follow the footpath on the other side of the hedge. When the footpath ends return to the road.

4. Continue along the road until it ends at a T-junction. Cross the road and continue ahead along New Cut (slightly to the left).

5. In about 600m at a T-junction, turn left, pass a row of houses, cross over Busbridge Road and continue along Stockett Lane.

6. In 100m you reach a tarmac passing point on the right; take the footpath in the corner. This brings you to a group of mill cottages. Turn left along the road and in 100m turn sharp right along a gravel path with an information board about the Loose Valley.

7. A little further on, open the kissing gate to enter the first field. Ignore a path that veers towards the garden fence and then keep to the path on the right. At the end of the field, go through a kissing gate next to a wooden fence.

8. At the end of the second field walk through the gate on the right and along a footpath between fences, after which you pass a house and later enter another field via a kissing gate.

9. 100m from the end of this field, there are two field gates on the right (one behind the other). Go through the kissing gate just to the left and continue along a gravel road for 200m. Then turn right along the track, passing in front of Kirkdale Cottages.

10. At the end of the track turn left along a concrete causeway that divides the village millpond.

11. When you reach the end, turn right towards Coxheath and take the first right up Church Street. When you pass the church, follow Church Street as it bends left. Cross the road at the top and ascend the stone steps ahead.

12. Continue on this footpath through orchards for 600m.

13. When the path (now a farm road) bends right, go straight ahead through the gap next to a field gate (Ignore the absence of a 'straight on' footpath sign - it does exist). In the orchard, a tall field hedge should be on your left and apple trees on your right. Continue ahead when the wide farm track bends to the right. When you reach houses on the left, continue on the path between garden fences and a wire fence.

14. Turn left along the road. When you reach the A road, turn left to cross this road at the pedestrian crossing. Then immediately turn right to cross Heath Road and walk ahead along Linton Hill for 200m. Turn left onto a footpath just before the pavement runs out.

15. When the path ends at a kissing gate turn right along the tree-lined drive.

16. At the gate of the Palladian manor turn right (keep the fence on your left). In 300m go through the churchyard and exit onto a cobbled path down to the road.

17. Cross the road and enter the Bull Inn pub car park. In the far right corner you'll find the footpath. In 100m descend steps to a road. Follow the road round to the right.

18. In 400m turn right up the road. Go under the footbridge and immediately up the stairs on the left. Turn right (not over the footbridge) to join the Greensand Way, which you now follow until the end of the walk.

19. In 900m cross the road to rejoin the Greensand Way.

20. Continue along the path and after the oast houses and barns follow the farm track as it bends left. When you reach a field gate turn right before the field gate to continue along a fenced-in path.

21. The path bears to the right and quickly left. On your right are coppiced chestnuts.

22. When you come out into orchards, a farm track joins from your left; continue in the same direction at the same height along the track, ignoring a track that forks to the left.

23. You eventually descend steep stone steps to a road. Turn right along the road and in 100m turn

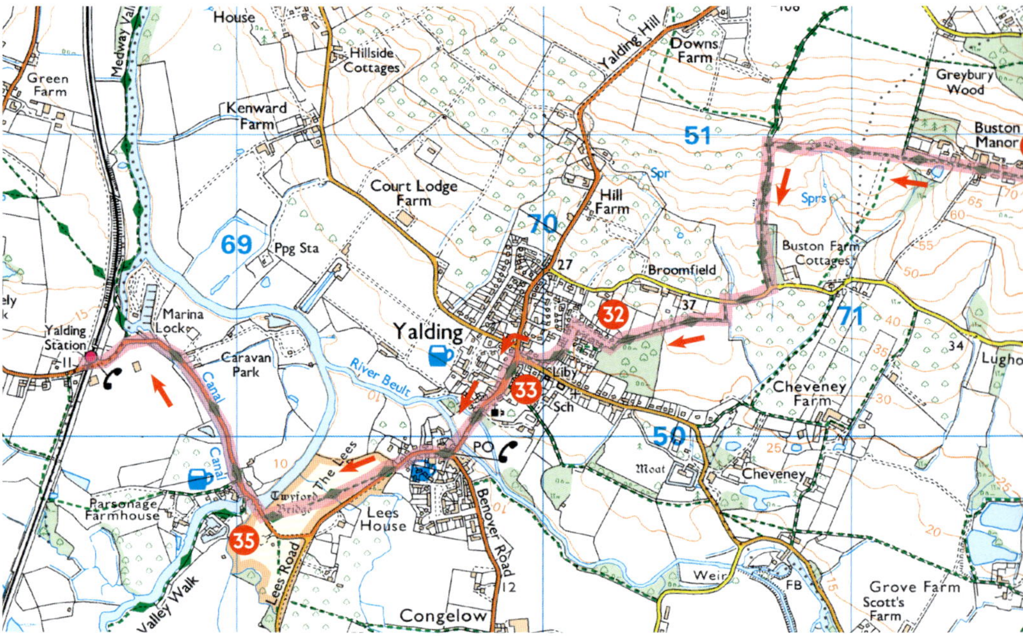

left up the bank to join the easily missed footpath.

24. Turn left and follow the footpath round to the right around the bottom of the orchard.

25. Halfway along this first orchard, just after the hedge comes to an end, go through a gate on the left and turn right to continue on the Greensand Way. The orchard you should be walking through is no longer there.

26. As you reach the oast house turn left along a footpath that circumnavigates the gardens and continue along a track. When it ends turn right onto the road.

27. In 150m, before the road bends left, take the hidden footpath on the left.

28. The path runs through woodland and then bears left down a flight of steps.

29. Turn right along the top of the field and then follow the field edge downhill. When the woods on your right finish, continue ahead across the field. When you come to a wooden footpath post (about level with the Manor House on the left), turn right.

30. In 500m you come to a road, continue straight on towards the oast houses. Go past the oast houses and past a metal bar gate, with buildings on the right.

31. In 700m turn left down the holloway. At the end turn right onto the road. In 150m turn left onto a footpath that soon bends right with tall garden fences on your right. This eventually brings you out into a residential road.

32. Turn right along this road and follow it round to the left. Ignore the turning on the right. Just as the road bends to the left again, turn right into the parking area and along the footpath signposted Greensand Way.

33. The path eventually merges with Vicarage Road. At the T-junction, turn left along the main road, walk through the village and over the longest medieval bridge in Kent.

34. At the T-junction, turn right. After the last house, turn half-right onto the footpath across Yalding Lees. The footpath soon forks; follow the left fork across the Lees.

35. When you rejoin the road, turn right over the bridge and continue along this road for 1km (passing to the right of the environmental agency building) until you come to the station.

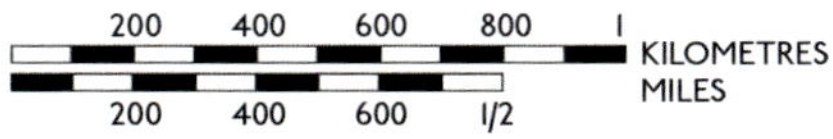

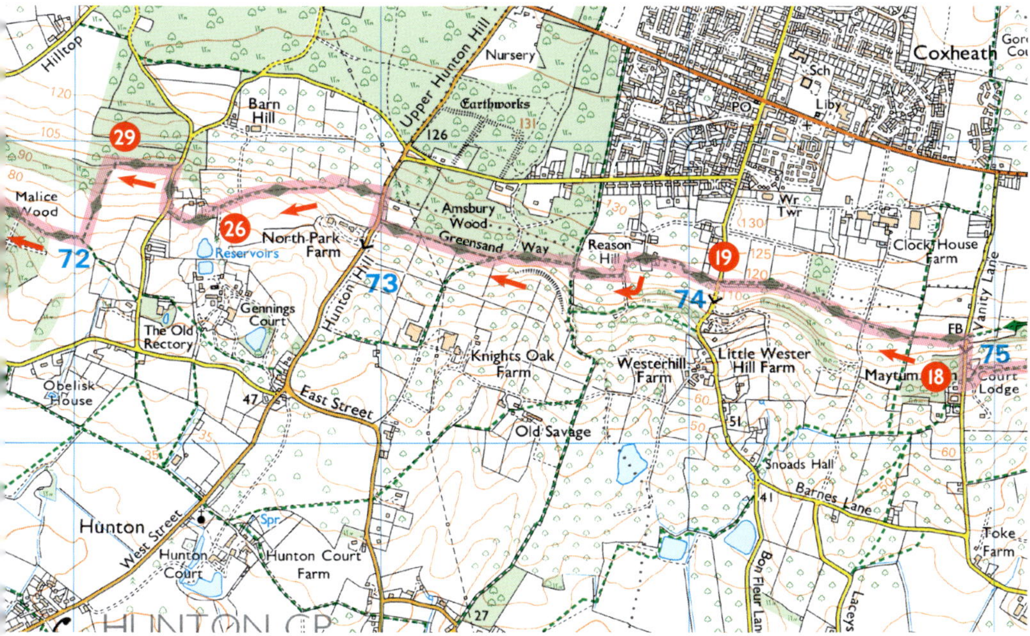

RICHMOND CIRCULAR, LONDON

Deer, hard with muscle, lower their heads and lock antlers.

They push and circle, unlock and clash again, the sound of bone on bone carries across the park. The rut is another autumn event worth making an effort to see, slightly scary but captivating.

October is perhaps the best month to see fallow deer and red deer rutting. And Richmond Park has both. The best time is early morning or evening; during the day you can be unlucky and see nothing, but at other times you'll experience plenty of this annual ritual in the middle of the afternoon. Just keep 50m between you and the deer and 100m if they're engaged in a rut. If you want to see a bit of autumn colour as well, wait until the end of October.

During the rutting season, the large herds of red deer split into smaller groups, each dominated by an alpha male. If you stop to watch the spectacle unfold you'll notice the dominant stag will now and again sniff and harass a hind. The hinds never seem keen on the attention and run ahead. Younger stags may wait and watch on the periphery and make occasional forays into the group, hoping to mount unnoticed. The older stag usually spots them, bellows and chases them off and then returns to a high point to survey his herd.

Even without deer, Richmond Park is impressive. Wild, sweeping expanses of rough grass are interspersed with patches of woodland and stand-alone ancient trees. While England may be one of the least wooded countries in Europe, ironically we possess more ancient trees than most. Green woodpeckers fly low across the grass to safety. Stonechats, with their distinctive black heads, white collar and orange breasts, sit brazenly on bracken, and flashes of blue, white and pink give away the jays, active at this time

INFORMATION

BEST TIME: October

LENGTH & DIFFICULTY: 8 miles (13km); easy, no stiles, one gradual ascent and descent

APPROXIMATE TIME: 4 hours

TRAINS: Richmond station in zone 4 brings together the District line, London Overground and National Rail. From Waterloo (on National Rail) as little as 16 minutes. Use contactless or a pass

MAP: OS Explorer 161 (London South)

FOOD & DRINK: Pembroke Lodge, about a third of the way into the walk. The Teahouse at Petersham Nurseries is two-thirds into the walk (Wednesday to Sunday until 4:30pm); lots of places to eat in Richmond

PICNIC: Plenty of benches – just below Pembroke Lodge (with views), elsewhere in the park or along the Thames

TOILETS: Richmond station, the car park next to Pembroke Lodge, at the Isabella Plantation and at the Petersham exit of Richmond Park

of year as they seek out and store acorns. Serious Lycra-clad cyclists shoot along the cycle paths and hundreds of visitors on foot are somehow absorbed. London feels very far away, although the peace is interrupted by gangs of parakeets and frequent low-flying planes coming into Heathrow.

While this circular walk from Richmond station is designed to give you a fair chance of seeing the deer rut, it packs in much more. Early on you cross Richmond Green, the jousting ground for the Tudor Royal Palace, whose residue you pass in Old Palace Yard. The walk takes in two of London's protected views: the first from the 18th century terrace on Richmond Hill – the famous view of the Thames and Petersham Meadows protected from development by the Richmond, Ham and Petersham Open Spaces Act of 1902. At least one of Turner's paintings of this scene is displayed at Tate Britain. The second is from King Henry's Mound in Richmond Park. From here you can see one of London's eight protected views of St Paul's. The cathedral can be seen with the naked eye, at the end of a gap cut between trees, but more clearly through the telescope on the Mound. Unfortunately a 42-storey tower block in Stratford, behind the dome, now destroys the pristine outline of St Paul's.

Turn around here to see a panoramic view of the Thames Valley with Windsor Castle in the distance. The same view can be enjoyed at leisure from the cafe terrace at Pembroke Lodge or over a picnic on the benches below the Lodge.

Towards the end of the walk, there's a long stretch along the Thames, which is still tidal here and floods the Thames Path at Richmond when tides are high. A clutch of boat builders hang on near Richmond Bridge, each with a cavern under the arches. You can watch them restoring long wooden rowing boats, wherries and skiffs, some more than 100 years old. Richmond itself provides an opportunity to enjoy shops for the well-heeled.

DIRECTIONS

1. Exit Richmond station and turn left. Almost immediately cross the road at the pelican crossing and go straight ahead into Old Station Passage.

2. Turn left at the end of the passage. When you reach Richmond Green, take the path diagonally across the Green, crossing a road halfway, and aim for the red postbox on the far side.

3. Cross the road and go straight ahead and under the arch. Aim for the far-right corner of Old Palace Yard and exit via a lane, passing white bollards with the letters ER. At the road turn left and continue until you reach the Thames, where you turn left along the river towards the bridge.

4. At the bridge, ascend the stairs on the left. Cross the road at the zebra crossing ahead, continue in the same direction, turn right at the mini roundabout and cross this road at the zebra crossing and continue uphill.

5. After the shops on your left, cross the road and continue uphill. In about 150m, just before a line of low metal railings, turn right between two brick gateposts and immediately left along the walkway above Terrace Gardens; follow this until it ends.

6. Continue along the road until you reach a zebra crossing, which you cross to reach a triangular island. Bear right and over the next zebra crossing. Turn right along the pavement and enter Richmond Park.

7. Once inside the park, just before you reach the small roundabout, turn right to cross the road and walk on the path ahead, with the fence just on your right.

8. In about 400m, just before a tiny brick building, turn right through a gate with a Royal Parks Pembroke Lodge sign on the front.

9. Continue ahead and under the trellis of the Laburnum Walk. When the path forks, take the left fork and then very quickly a right fork. Continue ahead and bear right uphill to King Henry's Mound.

10. Carry on in the same direction to come off the mound. When you reach a footpath crossroads, turn right signposted to Pembroke Lodge. At the end of the yew hedge, take the middle of three paths and continue until you come to Pembroke Lodge, where you bear left along its side and then right to reach the entrance.

11. Unless you're stopping here for lunch or a picnic, turn left and exit via the gate, walk through the car park, cross the road, walk across grass for 25 metres and turn right along a wide track.

12. In 100m turn left at a crossroads along a tarmac road. At end of the tarmac road the path forks; take the left fork, which later passes through a wood.

13. In 800m, when you emerge from the wood, continue ahead at a five-way footpath junction. In 200m (having ignored a footpath crossroads in the grass) turn right along a wide gravel and sandy track.

14. After walking between two lakes follow the path to the right along the edge of the lake.

15. Follow the path as it veers away from the lake and through some trees. Cross over a ditch. At the first fork take the right path and at the (closely following) second fork take the left branch away from the fencing and follow this out of the trees and through an open area of bracken.

16. Follow this path straight ahead for about 500m, until you come to the edge of the fenced-in Isabella Plantation. On your way cross a tarmac road, a footpath crossroads and a wide sandy bridleway.

17. When you come to the plantation follow the fence round to the right. In 300m enter the plantation through the first metal gate in the fence.

18. The path forks almost immediately; take the right fork past the information board. The path isn't very clear, so head for the bench about 100m in front. Then turn left along the path in front of the bench and ignore turnings off to the left and right until you come to Thomson's pond.

19. Turn right over the tree trunk stepping stones and right again along the path away from the pond. Follow this path, ignoring turnings off to left and right, until you come to a footpath crossroads.

20. Turn right following the signs on the tree trunk to Pegs Pond Car Park (290m); again ignore all turnings off to the left and right until you reach a large pond and follow the exit signs left over the bridge.

21. Exit to the right of the toilet block, walk across the car park and follow the tarmac road.

22. In 200m cross another tarmac road and walk ahead onto a grass path.

23. In 100m cross a ditch. The path forks; take the right fork, walking towards the house with the red tiled roof about 300m away.

24. At a footpath crossroads continue ahead. About 150m from the house follow the path as it bears left through some scattered trees. Come level with the house and continue straight on to come to a pond.

25. Go left round the pond, then straight ahead and turn left along a tarmac road. Walk straight ahead, aiming for the brow of the ridge, crossing the main road and ignoring other paths.

26. When you reach the ridge turn right on the path just below the brow and in 150m, at a two-armed footpath signpost, descend the steps. Follow the Capital Ring signs until you leave the park. The route continues high up for quite a while. As you near the end of the park turn left downhill along a wide grass path with benches to reach the exit.

27. Turn left when you come out of the park and cross the road at the pedestrian crossing. Turn right and then left down an alleyway just before the bus stop, signposted to the River Thames.

28. At the end of the alley turn right along a gravel drive and then follow the lane round to the left (ignore the white footpath sign to the Thames). When you reach the entrance to the garden centre turn right into a small turning area and over the stile on the right. Turn left to cross Petersham Meadows and continue ahead to reach the Thames. Go through a kissing gate and turn right onto the Thames Path.

29. In 400m the Thames Path bends right. In 50m after this turn left through a kissing gate and through a small park next to the Thames. Continue on the Thames Path for another 800m and walk under the bridge. Aim for a white building ahead – the White Cross pub.

30. When you reach the pub, turn right up Water Lane. Then turn left along George Street, which you follow as it bends right. In 500m you reach Richmond station on the right.

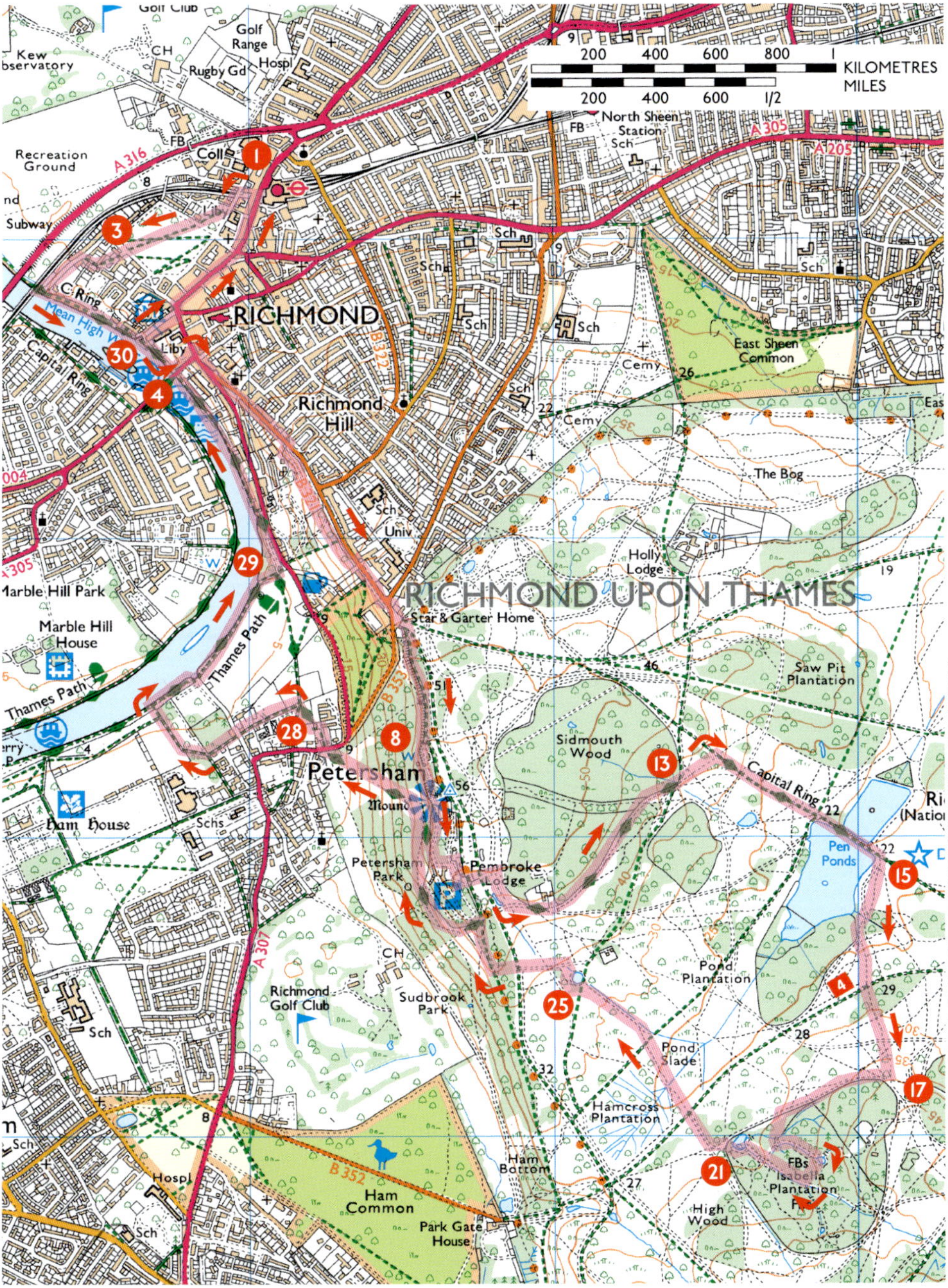
200
400
600
800
1
KILOMETRES
MILES
200
400
600
1/2
Kew Observatory
Golf Club
Golf Range
Hospl
Rugby Gd
Recreation Ground
Subway
RICHMOND
Richmond Hill
Capital Ring
North Sheen Station
East Sheen Common
The Bog
Holly Lodge
RICHMOND UPON THAMES
Star & Garter Home
Marble Hill Park
Marble Hill House
Thames Path
Saw Pit Plantation
Sidmouth Wood
Petersham
Ham House
Petersham Park
Pembroke Lodge
Pen Ponds
Richmond Golf Club
Sudbrook Park
Pond Plantation
Pond Slade
Hamcross Plantation
Ham Bottom
Isabella Plantation
High Wood
Ham Common
Park Gate House

Walk 17

SEVENOAKS CIRCULAR, KENT

The glow of a brazier and the smell of roasted chestnuts on a chilly evening are now rarities on the streets of London.

Chestnuts foraged in woods around the capital are smaller than the imported street fare, but for me autumn wouldn't be the same without them. Roasted in the oven, the sweet waxy nuts are more delicious for the effort of gathering them.

The chestnut season is reasonably long, from the end of September to the beginning of November. However, the peak time is short and usually falls in the last two weeks of October. Too early and many nuts are white, too late and they're squidgy or hollow. By mid October the ground is littered with their green hedgehog cases. Many are beginning to split, as the plump, burnished nuts push through the cupules.

The sweet chestnut is our honorary native tree; they originate from the southern Mediterranean and it's claimed they were brought here by the Romans 2,000 years ago, although others argue they arrived in the 16th or 17th century. Luckily for Londoners, these trees thrive in the south-east. Particularly rich pickings are to be had in Kent and Sussex, as they were planted en masse in the 19th century to provide poles for hop fields.

While plenty of walks have sweet chestnut trees, this one in Knole Park has an avenue named after them – Chestnut Walk, planted out in the 18th century. The price you pay for your chestnuts is 1km of road walking along Sevenoaks' main street and back again to the station, although the quaint shops and pubs partly compensate. But once in Knole Park you reach full-blown countryside. The National Trust's Knole House sits in the middle of Kent's last medieval deer park and one of Henry VIII's hunting grounds. Around 350 wild sika and fallow deer roam across acres of wild wood

INFORMATION

BEST TIME: Last two weeks in October

LENGTH & DIFFICULTY: Main walk 8½ miles (14km). Shorter option 6 miles (9.5km). Longest option 10½ miles; easy but with one easier type stile and one climb on the longer walks

APPROXIMATE TIME: Main walk 4¼hours. Shorter option 3 hours. Longest option 5¼ hours

TRAINS: Charing Cross to Sevenoaks (weekends twice an hour, weekdays frequent; from 33 minutes). Buy a day return to Sevenoaks

MAP: OS Explorer 147 (Sevenoaks)

FOOD & DRINK: Knole House cafe or on the longest walk Ightham Mote cafe

PICNIC: Benches at One Tree Hill and a few in Knole Park

TOILETS: Sevenoaks station, Knole House cafe

pasture full of tussocky grass and clumps of veteran trees. Visit before the end of October, especially near dawn or dusk, and you may catch the deer rutting. Photographers with long lenses hang out at Echo Mount (**5** in the directions) to capture the stags that gravitate there. Here stags bag their rutting stands on higher ground.

Fungi seem to thrive at Knole too. Huge parasol mushrooms with their slightly scabby tops and ruff of deep gills beneath are the most obvious, but look closely and you'll find small brightly coloured wax caps hidden in the grass. The clusters of vivid yellow and blood-red wax caps are an uncommon sight in the south-east, as they only grow in nutrient-poor, herbicide-free, unimproved grassland.

The walk has a small extension, a 2½ mile loop along the Greensand Ridge and back via One Tree Hill, with sumptuous views across the Weald, a wooded landscape often misty at this time of year, with occasional fields of sheep and oast houses in the distance. If you want to stay out longer, keep going to Ightham Moat (another National Trust property) and return by the same route, along the Greensand Way (not marked on the map). On Sundays you can take advantage of a free shuttle bus back to the train from Knole House if it's operating.

DIRECTIONS

1. Go down the ramp as you leave the station and continue ahead along the busy London Road for 1km until you're well into Sevenoaks shopping area. Just before a zebra crossing turn left along pedestrianised Dorset Street.

2. At the end of Dorset Street, cross the road and turn right along the pavement. In 100m, turn left into Redman's Place (a short alley).

3. Walk through a small car park, cross the entrance to Waitrose car park and continue ahead into Webbs Alley. In 300m, right at the end, enter Knole Park.

4. Stay on the path ahead, cross the grassy ride and continue uphill until you come to a road with a sign that says: Please help protect the wildlife of the park.

5. Cross the road and go straight ahead on the path, which goes into bracken. You emerge onto the hillside and Knole House comes into view. Follow the footpath sign on the wooden post to the top of the hill (Echo Mount); aim for the clump of trees in front.

6. At the next footpath post among the trees, ignore the direction of the arrow and instead go downhill, keeping the car park on your left. You're aiming for the grassy footpath on the other side of the road.

7. Walk past Knole House and then alongside the high garden wall. When you reach the corner of the wall, follow the path as it bears left to keep following the wall.

8. When the wall ends, keep on the Greensand Way, which continues ahead, bends to the left and then into trees.

9. At a footpath crossroads with a tarmac path, continue ahead. In another 700m you reach a T-junction. The tarmac path running left to right is Chestnut Walk. Endless sweet chestnuts can be found under trees along here.

10. **For the longer walks** continue on the footpath ahead and in 100m exit the park through a metal gate. **For the shorter walk** turn left along Chestnut Walk and pick up the directions at **21**.

11. Cross the road and continue on the Greensand Way through the wood.

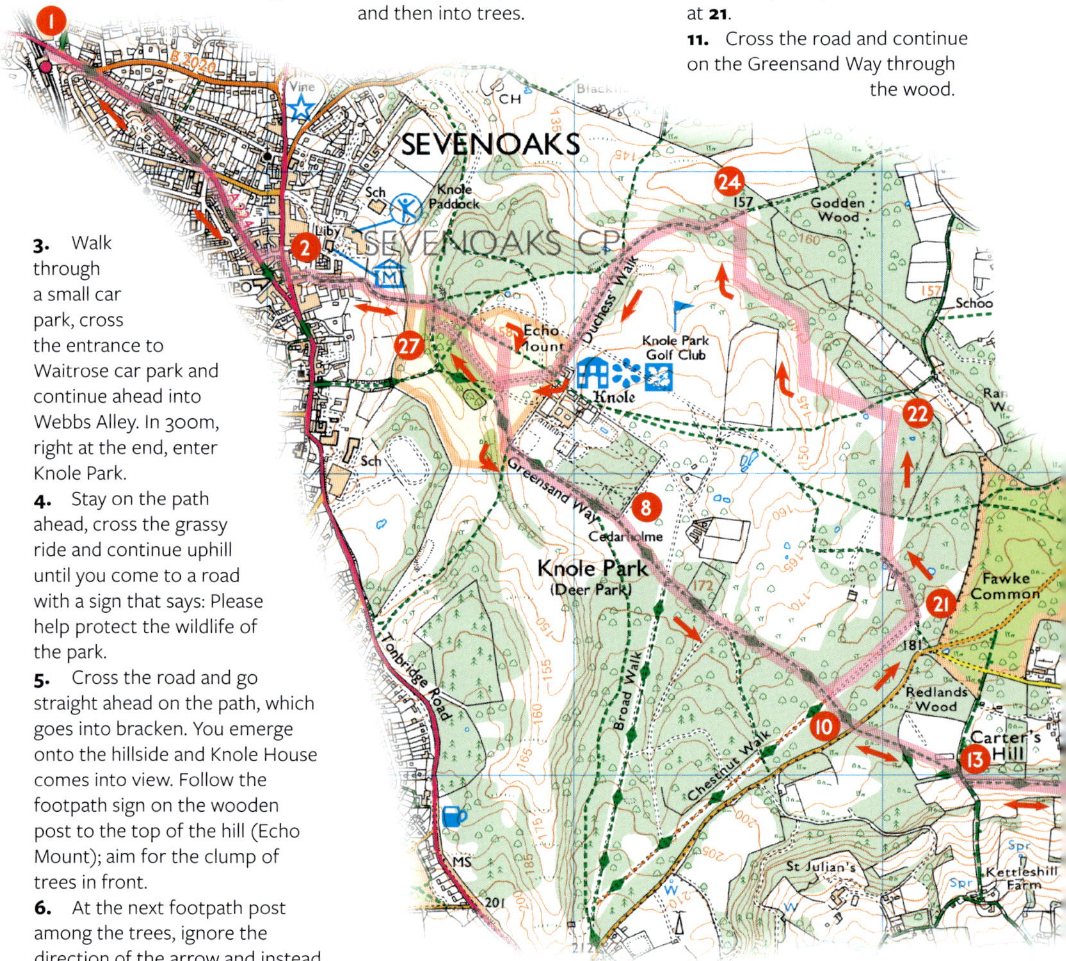

SCALE 1:25 000 OR 2½ INCHES TO 1 MILE 4CM TO 1 KM © CROWN COPYRIGHT 2021. OS 100063

12. Climb over a stile and into a field. Turn right along its edge and then turn left along the bottom edge. Go through the gate in the corner of the field.

13. Turn right along the footpath and in a few metres turn left to continue along the Greensand Way; lovely views of the Weald of Kent open up. After around 500m the footpath goes down a driveway to a road. Leave the Greensand way at this point. Cross the road and continue ahead along a tarmac road with a green footpath signpost and house on the left.

14. In 250m the footpath forks; take the left fork signposted to kennels.

15. After around 600m, turn left up a tarmac road. The walk will now loop back on itself. (If you want to walk for longer, take the first footpath on your right, the Greensand Way, to Ightham Mote, then back. Note the map doesn't extend to Igtham.) In 100m at Rooks Hill Cottage turn left up stairs to rejoin the Greensand Way.

16. In a few hundred metres you come to the National Trust's One Tree Hill. Ignore the first turning on the right, then when the path forks take the left fork, keeping close to the escarpment edge. At the top of the hill there are benches and views across the Weald.

17. Continue along the Greensand Way as it descends to a road. Turn left along the road. In 100m walk up Shepherds Mead driveway on the right and just before the white gate turn right onto the Greensand Way.

18. When the path ends, cross the holloway, go through the gate (slightly to the right) and back into the field.

19. Walk straight ahead along the bottom edge of the field, then turn right and follow the edge of the field with the woods on your left. Go halfway along the field edge and follow the path into the woods and over a stile.

20. Walk through woods until you reach the road, cross this and enter Knole Park. Continue ahead and then turn right along the tarmac Chestnut Walk.

21. In 500m turn left along a tarmac path. You'll pass a red-tiled keeper's cottage. Just after the pond on the left turn right onto an unsignposted grass path.

22. After an open section the path runs next to a pinewood (on your right). About 150m before you reach woodland in front of you, with a short wooden post on your right, the path faintly forks. Take the left fork along another faint grassy path; you shortly pass a dew pond on your left.

23. Continue downhill until you reach the bottom of the valley and turn right along the grass ride. When you come to a sign, 'Warning Danger Golf Course ahead– golfers playing from the right', turn right uphill.

24. Near the top of the hill you meet a tarmac path; turn left here to return to Knole House.

25. When you come to the buildings turn left for the cafe, otherwise turn right and continue straight ahead, with the main car park on your right (and space for a row of cars on your left).

26. Keeping to the side of the road; follow the road round to the right. After around 250m, turn right to follow the road with a no entry sign.

27. In about 250m when you see the 'Please help protect the wildlife of the park' road sign, turn left down the footpath. Continue ahead, retracing your steps out of Knole Park, up Webbs Alley, across the entrance to Waitrose car park, across a small car park and along the short alley to the main road.

28. Turn right along the main road and cross when you reach Boots, opposite the stand-alone old white building, to walk along Dorset Street. Turn right along the main road and walk the 1km to the station.

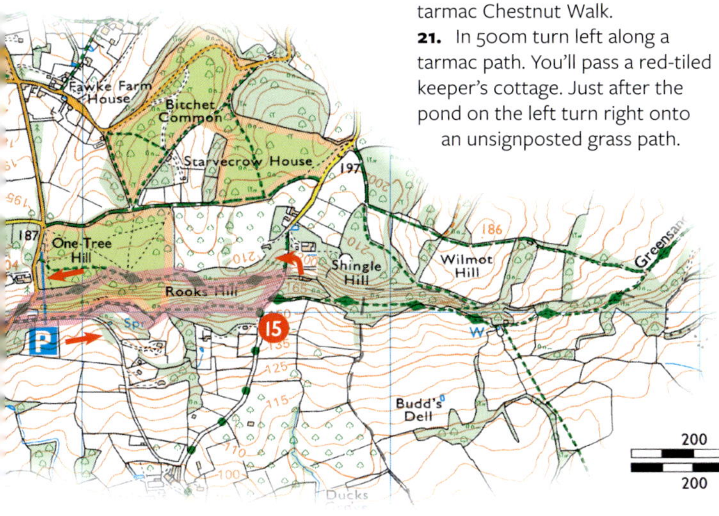

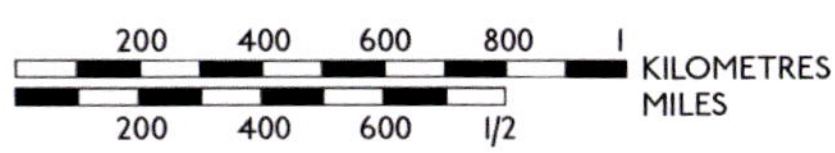

BENFLEET TO SOUTHEND, ESSEX

Wild salt marsh, a ruined hilltop castle and the best of Essex seaside.

This walk along the Thames Estuary is full of contrast and variety and firmly in the 'day out' rather than 'just a walk' category. As soon as you arrive you can spot curlews, redshanks and godwits busying themselves along the muddy banks of Benfleet Creek opposite the station. A little further and a melee of yachts and cabin cruisers fill the creekside, before you pass a super-stylish houseboat and Barge Gladys – a floating pub. Then, as the latch of the gate clicks shut, you're suddenly out in the open, striding across marshland under an endless sky, breathing deeply having escaped London's polluted air. Hadleigh Castle, 800 years old and a favourite of Edward III, is reached after a short climb. The craggy towers and the view of the Thames Estuary widening below are little changed since this scene was painted by Constable in 1828.

The views are wonderful; in the distance the delicate poise of quayside cranes mark the ports. On this side of the estuary you can see London Gateway, opened in 2013 and able to handle the world's largest container ships. On the other side are London Thamesport and Sheerness Docks. On a clear day you can make out fields of squat white cylinders and the chimneys and pylons of power stations, the paraphernalia of the Thames' edgelands. Across the creek is Canvey Island, birthplace of Dr Feelgood, forefathers of punk and now home to a growing community of Charedi orthodox Jewish families moving out of Stamford Hill.

You can spend a long time here, deciphering the thin line of Southend's pier – the longest in Britain, gazing at container ships sliding up and down the river and watching the toy-like trains below running between Fenchurch Street and Shoeburyness.

INFORMATION

BEST TIME: Last two weeks of October

LENGTH & DIFFICULTY: Main walk 7½ miles (12km); shorter option 5½ miles (9km); easy, one steepish climb and one more on the longer walk, one stile

APPROXIMATE TIME: Main walk 3¾ hours. Shorter option 2¾ hours

TRAINS: Fenchurch Street to Benfleet (at least twice an hour; from 39 minutes). Return journey takes a bit longer. Buy a day return to Southend Central for the main walk, otherwise buy a day return to Chalkwell

MAP: OS Explorer 175 (Southend-on-Sea)

FOOD & DRINK: Old Leigh pubs or Osborne Brothers for dressed crab and shellfish, Rossi's Ice Cream Parlour on Southend promenade, Van Looy's Fish and Chips opposite Southend Central station

PICNIC: On the grass at Hadleigh Castle or benches beside the sea from Leigh-on-Sea to Southend

TOILETS: All stations, Old Leigh harbour, Southend promenade

Returning to sea level you wander past Leigh-on-Sea's cockle sheds. Old Leigh with its cobbled street and small sandy beach is the nearest seaside for north-east Londoners and is full of pubs with seafood and sea views. Osborne Brothers serves up dressed crab, rollmops, oysters, brown shrimp and small piles of fresh cockles (far superior to the pickled variety). Cockles are unloaded by the ton from their boat Mary Amelia round the corner. Rows of dinghies are moored close to the quay and tilting yachts are scattered across vast mudflats. Trails of bird footprints crisscross the mud and groups of white seagulls sit between islands of golden grass.

A promenade walk finishes off the day, ending either at Chalkwell station or further along the esplanade at Southend. The walk doesn't take in the more garish Southend seaside and its famous pier, but a short detour will. Across the road from Southend's palm trees sits Rossi's Ice Cream Parlour, its decor little changed since the 1950s and one of my favourite places to stop. Glass panels above the counter advertise 'ices' 'Horlicks' and 'milk shakes'; polished stainless steel water boilers dispense tea and the menu still includes knickerbocker glories, alongside delicious ice cream. Finally, you wind up steep paths through terraced Cliff Gardens to Southend's handsome Victorian Clifftown next to the station.

This is a favourite walk of mine at any time of year. In summer I get to swim; in spring it's the only place I hear cuckoos; in winter it's full of migrant ducks and waders. But in autumn there's a special event. In October, Leigh-on-Sea welcomes the brent geese. Up to 4,000 of them land on Leigh's mudflats after a long and dangerous journey from the Arctic Circle. As they gobble eel grass you can hear their constant chat to each other.

Long bands of black rise up along the shoreline, as they momentarily fly up to stay ahead of the tide and when the sea finally covers their food, line upon ragged line of birds rise up. This is a gone-before-you-know-it spectacle, as the geese soon disperse across the Thames Estuary. To be sure of seeing them, get to Leigh around two hours before high tide, which means starting off at Benfleet about two hours before that. The RSPB and Leigh Town Council hold a Welcome Brent Geese event in October, when knowledgeable birders with telescopes help you get the most from your visit. Details are published online.

DIRECTIONS

1. From platform 2 descend the stairs and turn right along the underpass.

2. Exit the station, walk ahead, pass three bus stops and continue on the pavement until the road bends right across the creek. At this point walk straight ahead.

3. Ignore the Private Benfleet Moorings sign and continue on the public footpath through the gate and along the tarmac road next to the creek, passing Barge Gladys and ignoring a fork to the left. Follow the road until it curves to the left and ends at a gate. Go through the kissing gate onto a car wide track.

4. Follow this track on top of the causeway for 2km until you reach the first footpath sign, just after the first significant bend to the left. At this point turn left and walk down the embankment aiming for the stile ahead. Climb over the stile and make your way to the railway crossing in front.

5. Once on the other side of the train track take a slightly diagonal route to the right, aiming for a short wooden fence with a gap on the other side of the field.

6. Turn right on a gravel path. In about 600m, you reach a three-armed footpath sign (ignore a footpath to the left by the first signpost on the way). Take the short left fork, go through a kissing gate and turn left uphill. You soon join a wide stony track leading to Hadleigh Castle.

7. In 200m go through the gate in the metal palisade fence just after the English Heritage Hadleigh Castle board (not the second gate with public footpath signs). Walk across the lawn in the middle of Hadleigh Castle and

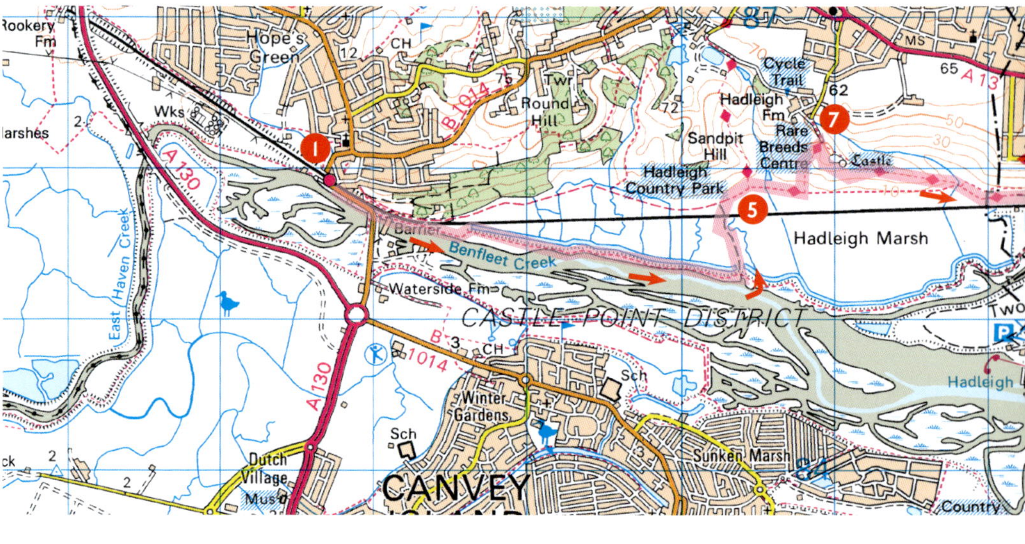

then over the wall between the two ruined towers.

8. Drop down the steep bank on your left and follow the path round to the right to exit the castle grounds via a metal gate and then immediately go through a kissing gate on your right.

9. Keep on the ridge path, which eventually descends to a kissing gate. Go through the gate and turn left onto a footpath and continue along the edge of fields for about 1km. When the footpath passes through small trees and shrubs, it becomes a car-wide tarmac path. At the road turn right along the pavement.

10. Turn right down stairs, just after the entrance to the first road and continue to Leigh-on-Sea station. Then turn right along the road towards the creeks and estuary. When the station wall ends, cross the road and descend the first flight of stairs. Cross the road in front and follow it straight ahead, passing first Leigh Marina and then a series of cockle sheds on the right.

11. At the car park, turn right on the pavement and follow this round to the left next to the estuary. Keep to the waterfront as the path passes pubs and restaurants overlooking the sea. The path moves away from the waterfront along a cobbled lane, which leads to Old Leigh's main street. Turn right and continue until you come to a small sandy beach.

12. Keep on the seafront path for 2.3km, until you reach hidden Chalkwell station (behind the long high wall). **For the shorter walk** catch the train from here, walk up the ramp round the corner, over the railway bridge and turn left. Otherwise, follow the path round to the right and continue along the promenade for about 2km until you reach the palm trees along the front. Cross over the road at the zebra crossing just after the second set of palm trees, opposite the large Rossi's Ice Cream parlour. Turn right along the pavement. Ignore the steps up to Southend Cliffs Pavilion. In 15m turn left onto a tarmac path, up into the gardens.

13. You're aiming for Clifftown Parade, the road at the top. Ignore all turnings off to the left and right and keep straight on unless directed otherwise. When the path forks next to two stone plinths to the right, keep to the left. Later keep to the right of a large round bush in the middle of the path. As you continue straight on, you come alongside a metal fence, which you keep on your right. When the pavilion comes into view, take the first set of steps to reach it, pass in front and turn left to reach the road.

14. Turn right along the road. In 400m you reach a small park. Turn left just after the park. At the end, cross the road in front and continue ahead with a bowling green on your right. Turn right towards the church and then left in front of the church along Nelson Street. At the end of the road turn right. Continue ahead, crossing two roads, to reach Southend Central station.

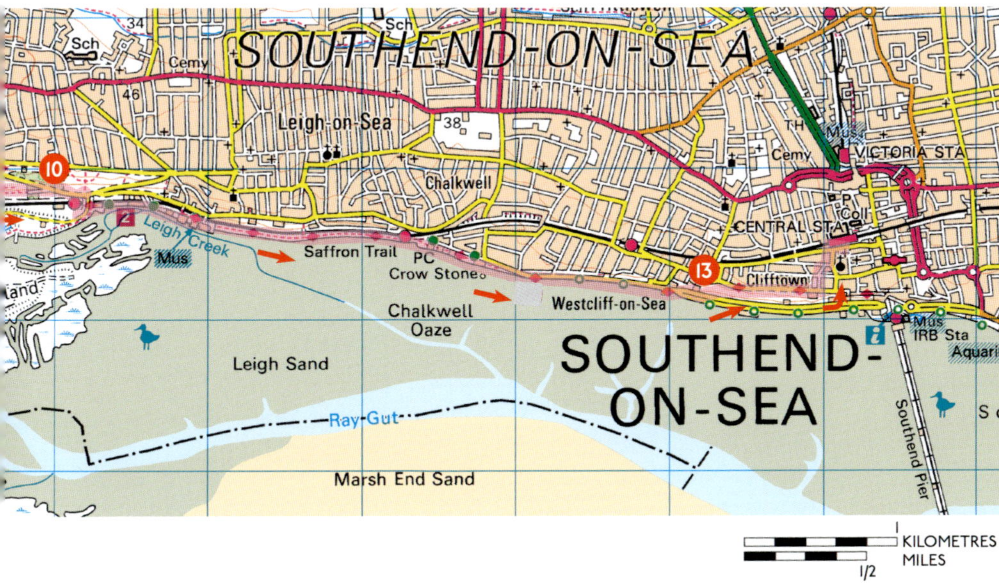

Walk 19

WENDOVER TO PRINCES RISBOROUGH, BUCKINGHAMSHIRE

A stunning walk along the Chilterns escarpment, the ideal length for short autumn days.

And a pub appears at just the right time along the way. The walk is along the Ridgeway, a national trail, and the route is so well signposted there's no need to constantly refer to directions or a map.

There are panoramic views of the low-lying Aylesbury Vale, washed out by the meltwater of the last ice age. The plain is now an agricultural landscape of large fields, very different from its wooded Weald counterpart on the other side of London.

This is one of the best places to watch red kites. They catch the updraft along the ridge for the sheer joy of it, coming almost level with you. As they steady or change direction, their tails tilt independently from their bodies as though remote-controlled.

Red kites soared above medieval London and dived from buildings ridding the filthy streets of carrion and were so valued they were protected by royal decree. But by 1880, across Britain, they had been hunted almost to extinction. The reintroduction of red kites to the Chilterns from 1989 is one of our success stories and they now number around 1,000 breeding pairs. They're even appearing above London again: I've spotted them above Alexandra Palace and Epping Forest.

The Chilterns is also one of the best places in England to see autumn colours. Down in the valley, specimen trees stand fire bright against the green fields, hedges are highlighted with yellow and woods are suffused with copper and gold.

But it is the monumental beechwoods that are the most dazzling. An army of smooth, straight trunks rise up from dense leaf mould, their branches silhouetted against layers

INFORMATION

BEST TIME: Last week of October and the first week of November

LENGTH & DIFFICULTY: 8.5 miles (13.5km); moderate, some steep ups and downs

APPROXIMATE TIME: 4¼ hours

TRAINS: Marylebone to Wendover (weekends hourly, weekdays twice an hour; from 39 minutes). Return from Princes Risborough to Marylebone (twice an hour; from 42 minutes). Buy a day return to Aylesbury, which covers both routes

MAP: OS Explorer 181 (Chiltern Hills North)

FOOD & DRINK: Buckmoorend Farm Kitchen just before Chequers (closed Mondays); the Plough at Lower Cadsden over halfway into the walk

PICNIC: Benches early on after Coombe Hill Monument, or overlooking Princes Risborough towards the end

TOILETS: At both stations

of luminous yellow with touches of bronze. Paths of russet leaves guide you through the autumn show.

Catching the best autumn hues is difficult. Each species of tree changes from green at a different time and shortly after they colour up, the leaves drop so their display is short-lived, and even shorter if there's wind, rain or frost. Variations in autumn temperatures complicate things further. To see the splendour of beechwoods, the first week in November is probably the safest bet.

Sadly this may not be a spectacle future generations will enjoy. Beech trees are particularly susceptible to drought, and if climate change means our summers will be drier, they may die out and will need to be replaced by the more drought-tolerant ashes and oaks.

While we have come to associate the Chilterns with beechwoods, they're a relatively recent phenomenon, planted in the 19th century to provide wood for the furniture-making industry. Bodgers worked in the woods, splicing and shaving beech into chair legs and spindles to supply High Wycombe's chair-making industry. Previously the Chilterns were covered in mixed woodland, which was coppiced to provide fuel for London.

A perk of this walk is having a snoop at Chequers, the Prime Minister's country residence. From Coombe Hill, Chequers comes into view in the valley below. The Ridgeway later passes right through the Chequers estate. Even though CCTV tracks your every move and fearsome notices announce that 'this is a protected site under Section 128 of the Serious Organised Crime and Police Act 2005', it's cheering that the path has not been rerouted away from the estate.

DIRECTIONS

1. Exit the station, turn right and walk up to the main road. Turn right and follow the road over the bridge. Turn right immediately after the bridge and walk over the HS2 bridge, up the small hill, cross the road at the zebra crossing and take the first left (note: Ordnance survey haven't at time of print updated their map with HS2 or the new road layout).

2. As the road bends left turn right onto the footpath, signposted the Ridgeway.

3. The path soon forks. Take the right fork through the kissing gate and walk uphill. The walk is along the Ridgeway long-distance path. The path is well signposted (sometimes only the picture of an acorn – emblem of a national trail – appears) so only brief directions are included. You can either follow the Ridgeway signs until Princes Risborough (and then go to direction **14**) or read on.

4. In 2km you reach Coombe Hill Monument. Walk in front of the memorial and keep to the well-worn path on the edge of the escarpment, passing some of the only benches on the walk.

5. In 600m turn right through a gate into a beechwood and follow the path for 300m until you come to a road.

6. Turn right and in 100m, next to a driveway, turn left into the woods again. The path runs near the top of the escarpment and after 800m descends. Near the bottom take the alternative path for walkers. Later bear left to reach the road (for Buckmoorend farm kitchen turn left at the road).

7. Cross the road and go into the grounds of Chequers. Walk across a field, a driveway, through two gates and across another field. Go through a gate and turn right. Walk along the edge of a wood.

8. Go through another gate and cross the middle of a green field. Don't be tempted to walk along the spurs to the right. Pass through another gate, and continue downhill. You pass a small hill (Chequers Knap) on your right.

9. Go through a gate and turn right along a holloway. In a few meters turn left up steps and walk through Grangelands and the Rifle Range, passing through a couple of gates and across a bridleway on the way.

10. At the bottom of the hill go through one of two gates and continue until you meet a road. Here turn left; the Ridgeway passes in front of the Plough pub.

11. Turn right after the pub up a steep hill. At the top there's a good view of Princes Risborough.

12. Follow the path on the left into the woods; in 400m you reach a road.

13. Turn right along the road and in a few metres turn left to reach a kissing gate, after which turn left to rejoin the Ridgeway. After around 200m the path forks. Take the right fork downhill towards a bench and stone pillar.

14. At the bottom (after steps and walking alongside a field), follow the Ridgeway path left, which takes you along the edge of Princes Risborough, past a playing field and alongside garden fences. Cross the first road you come to and continue along the Ridgeway for 1km until you reach a main road, passing a school on the way.

15. When you reach the main Wycombe Road, turn right. At the first traffic island, cross the road and bear right along Poppy Road. Turn left along Station Road, follow the road as it bends to the right. The station is next left as signposted. If you have a wait, pop into the Bird in Hand pub.

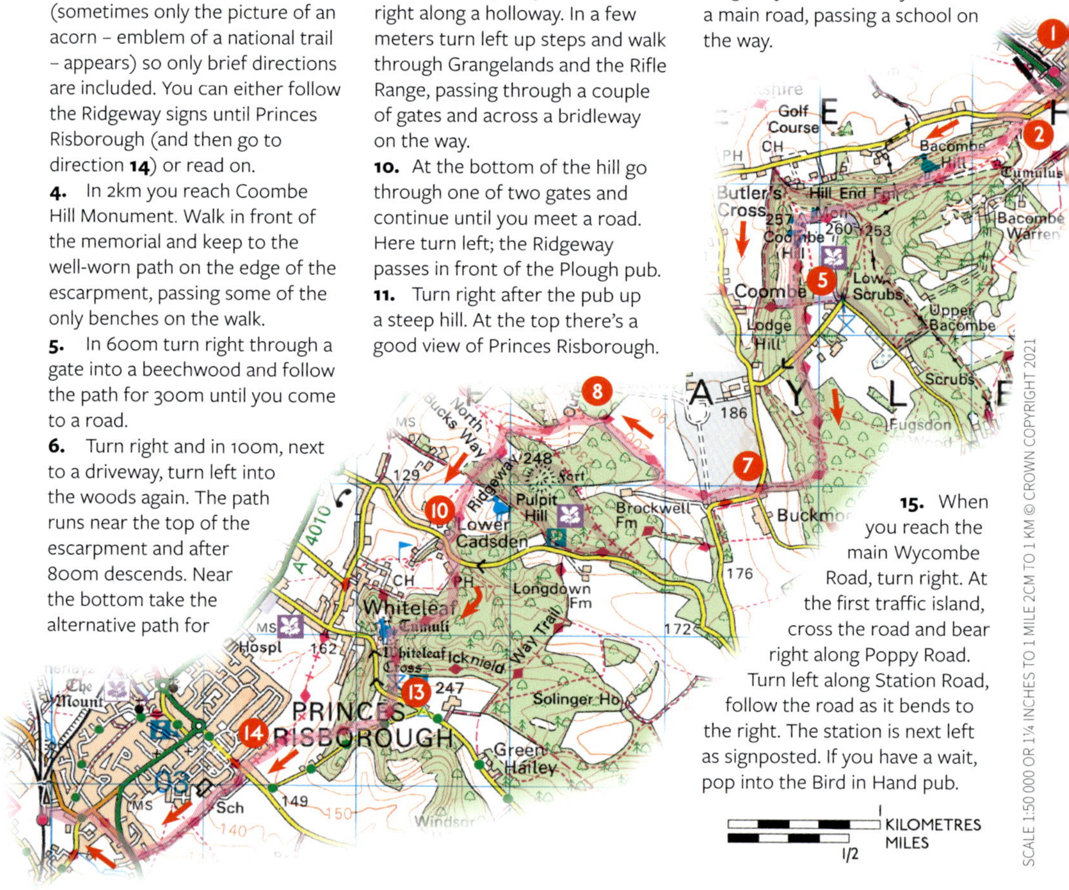

GUILDFORD TO CHILWORTH, SURREY

This is a walk up into the Surrey Hills through a landscape that seems made for this season.

You pass through various types of woodland, each with a slightly different autumn colour. A stand of pine is followed by oaks before you move through hazel coppice and onto silver birch, or sweet chestnuts with their slow swirl of fissured bark wrapped around their trunks and large serrated leaves scattered below. Oak trees are a tapestry of colour; silver birch shimmer their fine golden leaves, the wind puffing little clouds of them into the air. And then there's the yellow glory of a beechwood.

However, no matter how lovely they are, I get a bit bored just walking through woods. So emerging onto a grassy stretch along the top of the North Downs is a welcome change. There are fabulous views over low gentle hills, lines of ochre trees weave through evergreen plantations and fields of emerald green stand out in the forested terrain. All is framed by the thin misty line of the distant Greensand Ridge.

Picnic spots appear at just the right moment at the tip of a promontory and at St Martha's Church – the walk's highest point, where there are benches along the south side of the church, a peaceful place to enjoy the views and to bask in the sun if it's out.

After St Martha's you pass through more woodland. A particularly pleasing path gradually descends through the beechwood of Colyers Hanger. You catch the sound of water rushing along the Tilling Bourne below, before you see its glint. As you follow the course of the river, you pass lakes and unnaturally straight sections where the river has been canalised, interfered with to generate energy. The Tilling Bourne powered 24 mills that were used to produce gunpowder, to mill corn, make paper, tan leather or to forge

INFORMATION

BEST TIME: Last week of October and the first week of November

LENGTH & DIFFICULTY: 6 miles (9.5km); moderate, a couple of climbs up the North Downs, one steep, the other more gradual

APPROXIMATE TIME: 3 hours

TRAINS: Waterloo to Guildford (three times an hour, Sundays twice an hour; from 32 minutes). Return from Chilworth to Waterloo, changing at Guildford (hourly, Sundays less frequent; from 47 minutes). Buy a day return to Chilworth

MAP: OS Explorer 145 (Guildford)

FOOD & DRINK: Pub grub at Percy Arms Chilworth

PICNIC: Benches on the North Downs and later at St Martha's Church, all with views

TOILETS: Guildford station

iron. Towards the end of the walk you pass the ruins of gunpowder mills, the main industry in the area for 300 years. The valley, which is now so full of nature, was one of the most industrialised areas in the 17th century.

Fungi are of course another autumn treat and there is one place (**14** in the directions) on this walk where a selection of mushrooms is almost guaranteed. Look closely among the fallen oak leaves and you should see honey waxcap, brittlegills, fly agaric and the less showy oakbug milkcap. As a child, I found the desire to kick over fungi overwhelming, and I still feel a flicker of this strange urge. Our classic toadstool, fly agaric, with its bright red cap and white spots, always seems to suffer this fate.

But should I stop foraging for fungi? If you put fungi identification in a search engine, up pop guides and articles tempting you to look for edible mushrooms. Few voices encourage us to leave them alone – perhaps afraid of being labelled killjoys. But as we learn more about these ancient organisms, how underground their mycelium intertwines and penetrates the roots of trees, feeds them and connects them to each other, there is reason to think we should leave all their fruit, their fungi, to shed their spores. The vast quantities of mycelium underground is often hundreds, if not thousands of years old, releasing nutrients for insects and plants, helping to break down wood and other detritus – an invisible, essential component of our ecosystem. Over the next decade and beyond, our ecosystem will need all the help it can get, so perhaps supermarkets are the place to acquire fungi rather than our woodland.

DIRECTIONS

1. Exit Guildford station and turn right. Shortly before you reach the road, go down into the underpass. On the other side turn right up the ramp.

2. Walk ahead and follow the road to the left. Round the corner keep left rather than go over the bridge and aim for the High Street signpost. Descend the small flight of stairs on the right and turn right to walk along the river, the Wey Navigation.

3. Later don't turn left over the white bridge; instead turn left in front of the White House pub and then right to continue to walk next to the river.

4. At the next footbridge, turn right towards the Mill Mead sign. Walk along Porridge Pot Alley, then turn left along the road. When the road bears right, continue ahead but slightly left along Flower Walk. At the end turn left down an alley which takes you back to the Wey Navigation.

5. Turn right along the Navigation. In about 500m use the wooden bridge to cross the river.

6. Follow the path round to the left and then right signposted North Downs Way, initially across Shalford Water Meadows (take the left fork at the end of the meadows) and then straight across the playing fields towards the road.

7. Cross the road, following the signpost to Chantry Wood, and walk up Pilgrims Way. Take the third turning on the right along a wide path (signposted North Downs Way).

8. Turn right in front of the white house (leaving the North Downs Way) and immediately left through a car park. Continue ahead and walk up stairs and turn right at the top, continue uphill.

9. Pass the clearing on your left including Cathedral View and later take the first wide footpath on the right, which follows the contour of a steep slope.

10. In 300m the path forks at a Chantry Wood information board; take the right fork and go through a kissing gate and out of the woods. Turn left along the escarpment.

11. Continue through an open field gate next to a kissing gate, and turn right to follow the escarpment edge to a promontory with three benches, one in the shape of an oak leaf.

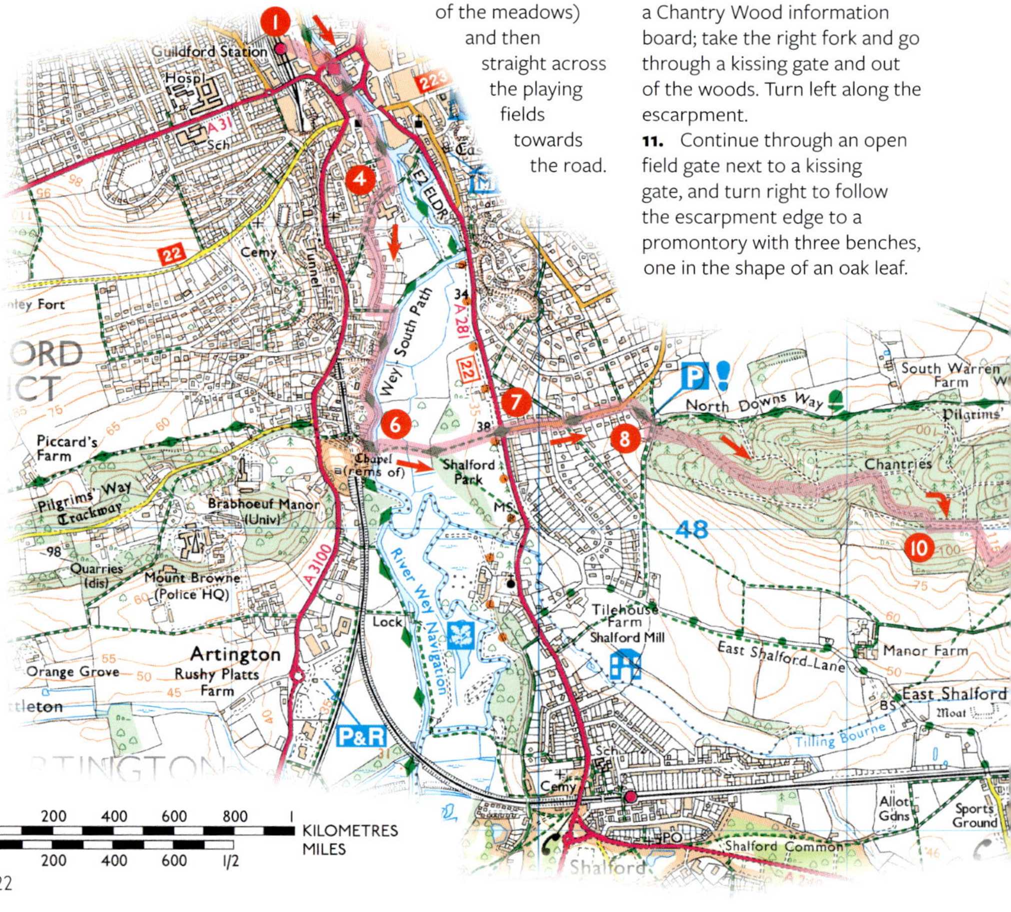

12. Continue along the escarpment edge, passing through a gate on your way; ignore paths that fork to the left.

13. Pass through another gate, shortly after take the left fork and go through a kissing gate into a camping field.

14. Walk diagonally across the field, aiming for the top right corner. On your way you pass two old oak trees, under which you should be able to find a range of fungi.

15. In the corner of the field, take the path into the woods to the right of a tap. Go through the wood and at a curved T junction turn slightly right, slightly uphill, to come out of the woods.

16. Turn left along the road. In a few metres turn right onto the North Downs Way.

17. Pass a few houses on the right and continue ahead along the North Downs Way for about 600m (ignoring turnings), until you reach St Martha's Church at the top of the hill.

18. Enter the churchyard and go past the church entrance to reach benches and views. There are more benches in front of the wall below.

19. Then turn left to exit the churchyard and continue along the ridge. As the path descends and keeps forking, keep to the main track close to the edge.

20. Ignore two signposted footpaths on the right (the second is just before a pillbox on the left and signposted Downs Link).

21. In a further 250m at a four-armed footpath post, turn right downhill. In 100m, at a footpath post, follow the path as it curves to the right. When you come to a large hilly field, turn left. In 800m you come to the bottom of the valley.

22. When you reach the lake, turn right onto the road; follow the road round to the right and walk alongside the river. Just after a second lake, turn half-right along a footpath with wire fences on both sides.

23. When you emerge into a grassy field, keep straight ahead alongside a ditch. Continue across the next field, leaving the ditch.

24. Turn right onto a car-wide track, over a stream and turn left through a gap in the fence. Walk along the footpath beginning with a Chilworth Gunpowder Mills information board. Go past the ruined buildings and continue along the path until you come to a clearing with picnic tables.

25. Just before the information board, take the footpath on the left, over a bridge and into Chilworth. When you reach the road, turn left and in 200 metres Chilworth station is on the right.

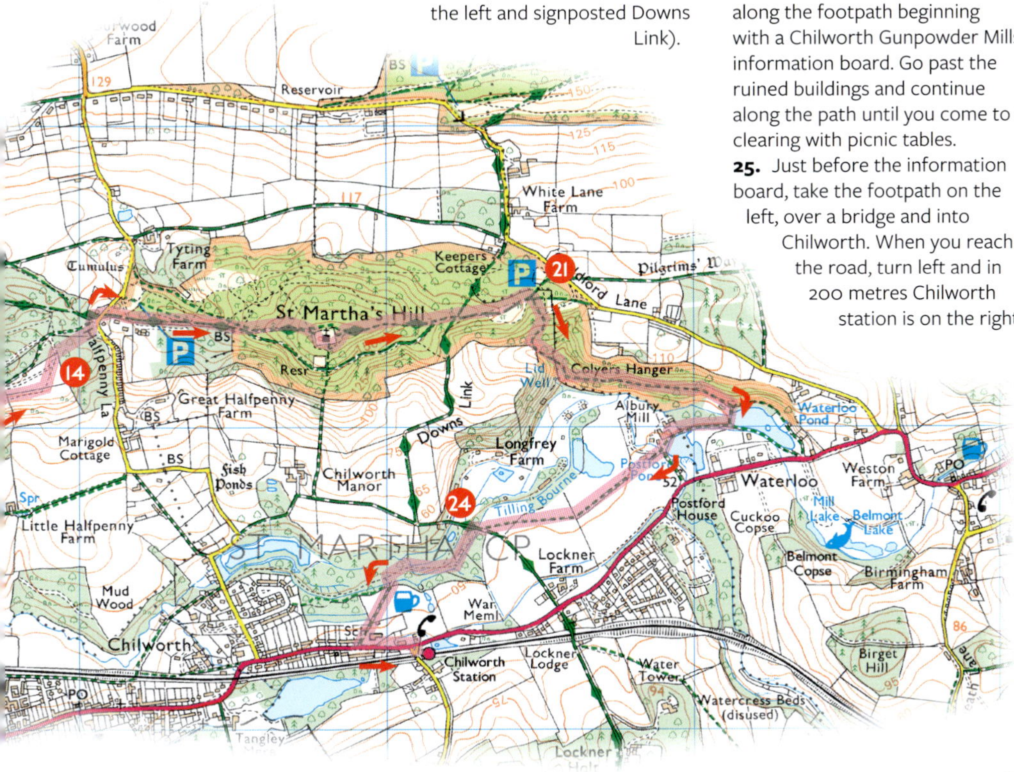

Featured winter walks

21 Faversham Circular: migrant waders and ducks
22 Falmer to Brighton: starling murmuration
23 Cookham Circular: Thameside walk
24 Harlington Circular: for snow or frost
25 Coulsdon Circular: for snow or frost
26 Box Hill Circular: catkins & winter trees

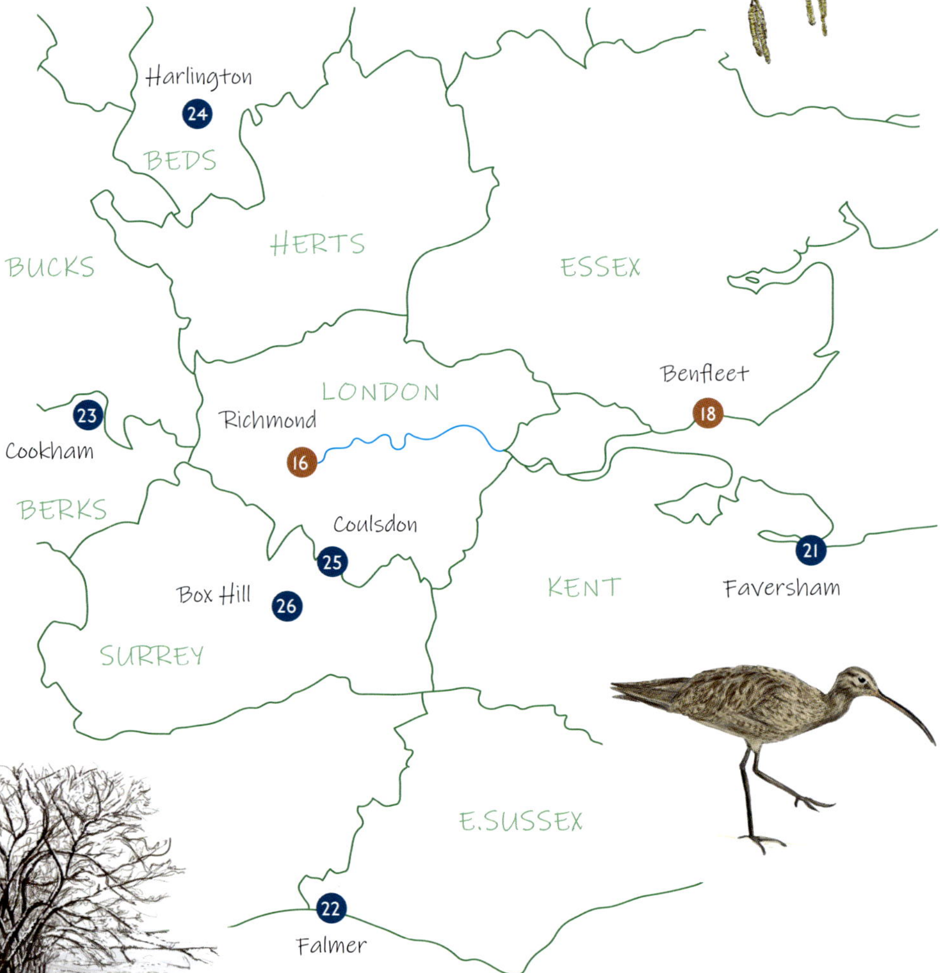

Other good winter walks

16 Richmond Circular: deer & Thames walk
18 Benfleet to Southend: migrant waders & ducks

WINTER

Winter, our least-loved season, still rewards those who venture out: bare trees inked magnificently onto the skyline, the wonder of walking through a landscape transformed by snow or just being out in the surprise brightness of February days.

Alexandra Harris points out in *Weatherland* (her survey of artists' and writers' treatment of weather through the ages) that nature in winter only began to be appreciated when homes were more effectively heated. Until then, images of winter were of inside scenes, drinking in the mead hall or sitting by the warm glow of the fire. The first known painting of snow in Europe was not until 1400. Historian Bridget Henisch concurs that winter 'was a season passionately detested in the Middle Ages. The traces of bare branches against a water-laden sky, the harmonies of black and grey and white, these were beauties still waiting to be discovered'.

But while all Londoners see winter trees, most won't have experienced the seasonal spectacle right on our doorstep. Each winter 300,000 birds migrate to the Thames Estuary, making it a site of international importance. Epic journeys are made from Siberia, Iceland and Scandinavia, and creeks, mudflats, pools, saltmarsh and scrubby fields become peppered with ducks, geese and waders. With luck you'll see skeins of honking geese, hundreds of roosting birds huddled at high tide or a late afternoon murmuration of starlings – swollen with the addition of winter migrants. The sad cry of curlews echoes across the marsh, lapwings' drawn-out peewits rise from the fields and oystercatchers' piping calls pierce the stillness as they fly off. It's an abundance to be treasured; a stark reminder of what we've lost elsewhere, in our woodland and on our farmland.

Each year I fall in love with winter a little more, but it remains my least favourite time to walk. I dislike miles of mud-trudging, when boots grow heavy with claggy clay, and while almost any walk is pleasant in spring, the same can't be said of this season. Identifying good winter walks is a challenge. They should display the best of the season, not be too muddy and finish with somewhere inviting to warm up – ideally a pub with a fire and good food. Brief December and January days also demand shorter walks closer to home. This is also a season when slightly obsessive use of weather apps pays off. Spot a sunny or snowy day in advance and reserve it for walking.

This selection includes two snow walks, a day out along the Thames Estuary, a seaside foray to witness a starling murmuration and rambles at Box Hill and Cookham, neither of which should be too muddy.

Walk 21

FAVERSHAM CIRCULAR, KENT

This is my favourite winter walk and if you like slightly desolate estuary landscapes you'll enjoy it too.

The route is exposed so wrap up warm and, if there's been rain, prepare for a bit of mud. If you have binoculars, don't forget to bring them. The walk starts in the ancient market town of Faversham, Whitstable's underrated neighbour. Pevsner described it as 'one of the most rewarding towns in the county, though pleasurable in many small ways rather than for spectacular beauties'.

As you step off the train from St Pancras, it feels like the 1950s. Everything is smallscale, the streets retain their independent shops and there's little modern development in the centre. Medieval timber-framed and white clapboard buildings are found along the way and the town is full of quirky architectural details. The market square is charming; the town's Guildhall sits above the old market. From here it's worth making a detour to see Abbey Street, described as 'the finest medieval street in southeast England'.

There's a mile of rather boring road-walking on the outskirts of Faversham to Oare, but then you're out in the open, walking along a creek and through marsh straight out of Great Expectations. Dozens of yachts are pulled up on the far muddy bank, their masts rare vertical lines in this flat landscape, and sometimes a Thames barge is moored along here, its red ochre sail bunched against its tall mast.

As you walk further out, you enter an immense landscape full of sky. Winter sun saturates the colours, a red buoy stands out against the steel blue water of the creek winding out to sea, gold marsh grass spills across brown mud dimpled with water, a reed bunting sways on a raft of silvered reed heads. Keep alert and you'll be rewarded with ornithological delights and occasionally seals. Oare

INFORMATION

BEST TIME: December to February

LENGTH & DIFFICULTY: 8 miles (13km). Shorter option with taxi from Oare to Faversham station, 6½ miles (10.5km); easy with some stiles

APPROXIMATE TIME: Main walk 4 hours. Shorter option 3¼ hours

TRAINS: St Pancras to Faversham (weekends hourly, weekdays twice an hour; 1 hour 7 minutes). Victoria to Faversham (twice an hour; from 1 hour 9 minutes). Buy a day return to Faversham

MAP: OS Explorer 149 (Sittingbourne)

FOOD & DRINK: The Castle or the Three Mariners (with a nice fire) both in Oare, 7 miles into the walk. Plenty of places to eat and drink in Faversham

PICNIC: Bench at the end of Oare creek by the hide

TOILETS: Faversham station

Marshes are an internationally important site for wetland birds. Numbers swell in winter when hundreds of waders from Russia and Scandinavia escape to its mild mudflats.

This is an excellent place to brush up on your birds and hone your birdwatching skills or just enjoy an occasional spectacle. As you stride out along the creek, redshanks scuttle along the mudbanks. Big fat curlews with their impossibly long curved beaks will be out on the mud and on the marsh. From the hide where the creek meets the Swale you often see a white line of avocets and a range of ducks and waders, pintails, godwits, teal, wigeon and shelducks. I've seen clouds of white waders disappearing and then reappearing as they turn in unison, and skeins of noisy geese. If you're lucky, a peregrine will scare hundreds of lapwings and plovers skywards in long black ribbons. You should certainly see kestrels and large marsh harriers. Sometimes you'll spot short-eared owls, hen harriers, sparrowhawks or merlins and towards dusk you could catch a murmuration of starlings.

At the end of the creek you walk along the Swale, a small strip of sea separating the mainland from the Isle of Sheppey. Then it's inland across rare grazing marsh and fields back to the village of Oare and its two pubs. Leaving Oare at dusk is okay as you're not reliant on daylight to walk back to Faversham and in December you'll have the benefit of Faversham's cheery Christmas lights to brighten your way to the station.

DIRECTIONS

1. At Faversham station walk down the stairs from the platform and turn right along the underpass.
2. Once outside turn left and walk across the zebra crossing in front of the Railway Hotel. Turn left and immediately right along Preston Street. In 200m don't follow the road round to the left when it becomes Stone Street; instead continue along Preston Street.
3. When you arrive at a T-junction turn left along Market Street. Pass the clock tower and medieval covered market on your right and continue along the pedestrianised street.
4. When you arrive at North Lane cross the zebra crossing and continue ahead down West Street.
5. Keep on the right-hand side of West Street. In 350m, with the Bull Inn on the other side of the road and a triangular grass traffic island in front, follow the road round to the right. In 100m you pass a large pond.
6. Take the next right up Davington Hill.
7. At the top you pass a road on the left with an information board in front of the church. Don't turn left here. Instead continue straight ahead along Priory Row. Follow this road for 1.2km until you come to Oare, passing housing estates and a turning to the M2.
8. Turn right just before the Castle pub. Follow the public footpath sign on the right through a kissing gate, walk diagonally across the field, pass through a gate on the other side and turn left onto the bank that follows the creek. If the weather has been wet this section can be very muddy.
9. Walk beside the creek for just under 3km until you reach a hide on a mini headland. Continue along the path, which now runs beside the Swale. In 600m cross a road, pass a brick building and go through a kissing gate to keep walking along the Swale.
10. In 1km turn left to walk around a crumbling jetty and go through a kissing gate (rather than follow the path round to the right) then continue straight on through a farm gate and head away from the Swale. Continue ahead on the path over grazing marsh. In 700m walk between two houses, then along a road until you reach a T-junction after 500m.
11. Cross the road and go through a gate to join a footpath. Walk straight ahead, pass through another kissing gate and along a path between wire fences.

12. When you reach a farm track, turn left. As the track bends to the left, continue ahead through the kissing gate and onto a footpath, which you follow across two fields until you reach a road.

13. Turn right along the road and in 50m turn left along a footpath. Follow the path across the fields to the top of the gently sloping hill. At the telegraph pole follow the path round to the right and continue until it ends at a road.

14. Turn left along the road. When you reach a junction go straight on into Oare. In 150m you'll be at the Three Mariners Pub. **For the short walk** book a taxi from here.

15. Otherwise continue ahead down Oare's main street. In 150m you'll pass the footpath along Oare creek, so from here retrace your steps. Continue along this road for 1.4km until it ends at a T-junction next to the large pond. Turn left and continue until you reach the road junction with a grass triangle that has trees in the middle and the Bull Inn behind. Turn left up West Street, cross North Lane to continue up West Street which becomes Market Street, pass the clock tower and when the road forks, go up Preston Street on the right. At the end of Preston Street turn left and cross the road to return to the station.

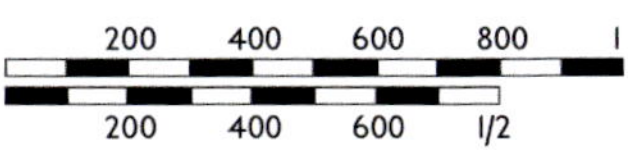

Walk 22

FALMER TO BRIGHTON, EAST SUSSEX

A decent walk up and over the South Downs and into Brighton to catch the breathtaking starling murmuration over the town's piers.

You start by climbing Falmer Hill, crossing flint-strewn fields and rough grassland edged by winter hedgerows. Small windswept hawthorns perch on the horizon and sleek black crows sit in the fields. After cooped-up London, it's liberating to be under a huge sky, inhaling lungfuls of fresh air. The downland chalk absorbs the rain, so the route isn't too muddy.

The headland of Selsey Bill is visible in the distance as you descend towards 'London by the Sea'. The urban sprawl of Brighton, Shoreham-by-Sea and Worthing runs along the coast, squeezed between the sea and the South Downs. From here, you dip in and out of Brighton's fringes, follow the racecourse, which forms a horseshoe along the top of Whitehawk Hill, and walk out along a finger of downland stretching to the sea. You then quickly weave through Brighton to enjoy a stroll along the sea front.

While this is an enjoyable walk, the main reason you're here is to witness the starling murmuration, one of the best in the UK. The days when 40,000 starlings congregated here appear to be over, in part due to milder winters, but they still gather in their thousands. In September migrant starlings begin to arrive from Scandinavia, Poland, Germany and Russia to join our indigenous flocks. From autumn the birds begin to roost en masse to combat cold nights and engage in the ritual murmuration before they bed down for the night. The murmurations reach their peak in December and January. In February the migrants begin to leave.

As dusk nears, thousands of starlings return from their feeding forays in the countryside and come together for a magnificent aerial display. Somehow they lose their pointed wings, beaks and tails in an enormous rounded cloud

INFORMATION

BEST TIME: December to January

LENGTH & DIFFICULTY: 6 miles (9.5km); moderate, two shortish steep climbs up the South Downs

APPROXIMATE TIME: 3 hours

TRAINS: Victoria to Falmer (twice an hour; 1 hour 32 minutes) or Thameslink via London Bridge (at least two an hour; 1 hour 27 minutes). All routes require a change at Brighton. Return from Brighton (at least twice an hour; from 1 hour 7 minutes). Buy a day return to Falmer

MAP: OS Explorer OL11 (Brighton)

FOOD & DRINK: Plenty of places to eat and drink in Brighton

PICNIC: Seafront benches and walls in Brighton

TOILETS: Falmer station then not until Brighton

that moves back and forth across the sky, seemingly in slow motion, with a wave-like momentum. The cloud expands, contracts and almost disappears as the starlings turn in unison, then – bang – it's back in black as they turn again. It splits and then re-forms, it pours down into twisted lines and then streams upwards. Towards the end, the murmuration moves closer and closer to the sea and the flock gradually diminishes as birds fly into roost on the lattice of iron girders beneath the pier. A starling murmuration isn't guaranteed; sometimes they just fly straight into roost in small groups.

The first time I sought it out, we waited expectantly, looking out to the remains of West Pier – an iron gazebo marooned at sea. A few small groups of starlings skitted across the water, but the sun set and there was no sign of a murmuration. Then suddenly we spotted a huge cloud of starlings above Palace Pier, further down the beach. Above us, flock after small flock rushed across the sky to join in. The spectacle lasted for over half an hour.

DIRECTIONS

1. Exit the station, turn left to go up the stairs and across the railway bridge. Turn left down the ramps toward the stadium. (If access to the stadium is blocked, it's possible to find a way through the university campus.) Continue along the road to the left of the stadium, which follows the curve of the building.

2. Ignore the road that turns off left. Instead walk up the stairs further on, to the coach park. Turn right along the side of the coach park to reach the road.

3. Cross the road and turn right along the pavement. When you reach the University of Brighton sign, turn left onto the footpath alongside a field. When you come to a large open field, turn right along the field edge.

4. At the end of the field, don't go through the gate. Instead turn left and follow the footpath uphill.

5. At the top, at a three-armed footpath post, turn right. On the way downhill, with Brighton ahead, go through the gate and walk along the footpath (with a fence on your left.)

6. When you reach the end of the field, go through the gate to the right of a field gate (with a dew pond on the other side) and continue on the track downhill, which leads into Bevendean.

7. When you reach a road, turn right (along the road) and near the bottom of the hill cross the zebra crossing.

8. Turn left up Auckland Drive. In 100m, when you come level with a group of trees on your left, cross the road then walk up the flight of steps and along the footpath.

9. Cross the road and climb up Fitch Drive. Turn left into the first road you come to, Dartmouth Crescent, and then turn left along Dartmouth Close.

10. At the end of Dartmouth Close turn right along the footpath, which takes you alongside paddocks and later becomes a car-wide track.

11. At the top, cross the road, then the next road, and go through the gate. Walk straight across the racecourse. Pass through a gate on the other side to exit.

12. Turn right along the grassy footpath, which follows the inside of the racecourse for 1.2km, aiming for the radio tower. After the grandstand on your right, the path ends at a road. Cross over and continue ahead on the path.

13. Shortly before the radio mast turn right at the end of the racecourse.

14. Before you reach the houses turn left through a gate onto another footpath. At the bench the path forks; take the right fork downhill.

15. After a small flight of steps turn left along a clearly defined path, which in around 500m will bring you out onto a road.

16. Turn right along the road and follow it down to the main road.

17. Cross the main road and continue down College Place until it ends at St Georges Road.

18. Cross over to follow Bloomsbury Place to the sea.

19. Cross the main road and turn right along the promenade. In about 150m descend the steps on the left. When you reach the lower level turn right to continue in the same direction. After around 1km you'll reach Palace Pier, where the murmuration is likely to take place (it can also take place over the derelict West Pier further along). The walled promontory after Palace Pier is a good place to watch the display.

20. To reach the station from the walled promontory, cross the main road at the pedestrian traffic lights and continue ahead along East Street (ignore left turns along King Road and Bartholomews) until you reach the main road (Castle Square).

21. Cross the main road and continue ahead along Pavilion Buildings. At the end, follow the footpath through Pavilion Gardens and past the beautifully lit Royal Pavilion. Take the second path on the left and follow this until you emerge onto a road, ignoring turn-offs along the way, and at a footpath crossroads, follow the sign to Brighton Dome.

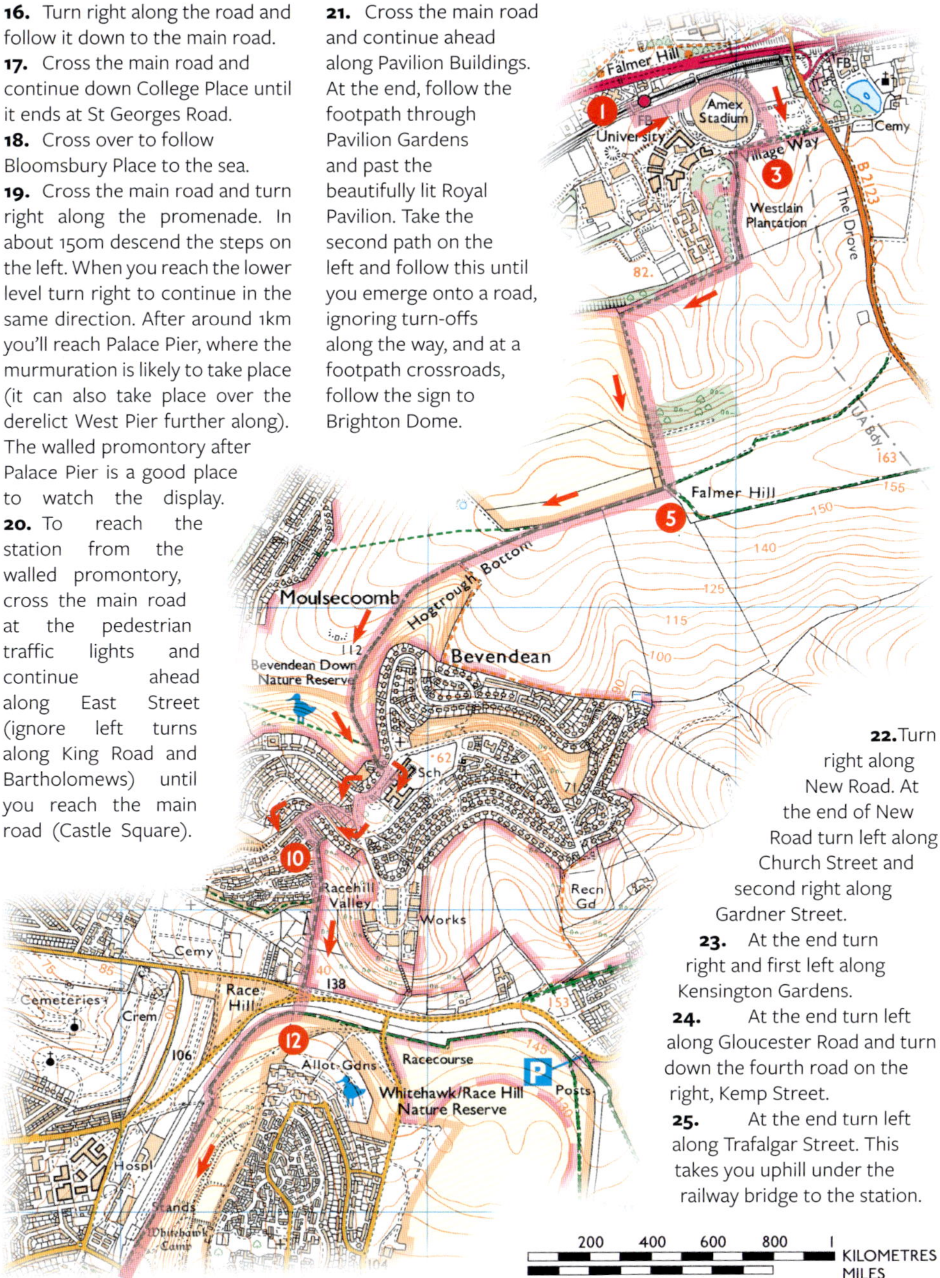

22. Turn right along New Road. At the end of New Road turn left along Church Street and second right along Gardner Street.

23. At the end turn right and first left along Kensington Gardens.

24. At the end turn left along Gloucester Road and turn down the fourth road on the right, Kemp Street.

25. At the end turn left along Trafalgar Street. This takes you uphill under the railway bridge to the station.

Walk 23

COOKHAM CIRCULAR, BERKSHIRE

This short circular walk along the Thames valley fits nicely into a winter's day.

There are views across the wide floodplain to the Chiltern Hills and almost a third of the walk is along the Thames, the stretch that inspired Kenneth Grahame's *Wind in the Willows*, or so it's claimed.

At the end of the walk there's enough day left to nose round Cookham, whose life and residents were immortalised in Stanley Spencer's biblical paintings. Spencer, who was born and lived here, described Cookham as 'a village in Heaven'.

This walk is very popular at weekends, so if you prefer not to catch snatches of other people's cheerful chatter or engage with their excitable dogs, venture out on a weekday if you can. It's not too long or too taxing, there are no stiles and the route is mainly flat apart from one steep ascent, which the shortcut avoids. After significant rain the Thames-side path may be muddy, if the ground isn't frozen. No particular aspect of winter is showcased on this walk, although there are a decent number of grand old trees, whose winter skeletons are rather wonderful.

It is one of those walks without any nasty bits. You are quickly out of Cookham and into fields. There is a satisfying section along the top of a chalk escarpment, where red kites course the currents at your height. Beyond is the thin line of the Thames, the river appears calm, but swollen with water, almost level with the marsh and sunlight glances off a row of white houses on the far bank.

You descend to join a strung out line of people walking along the river, wrapped up against the cold. As you walk along the Thames Path, it's hard not to gawp at the houses of Bourne End or peer into the houseboats, cabin cruisers and the more up-market yachts further along the riverbank. There's a rather quirky pub with Thames-side seating,

INFORMATION

BEST TIME: Throughout winter - December to first week of March

LENGTH & DIFFICULTY: 5½ miles (9km); easy apart from one steep climb that can be avoided (by following the shortcut shaded in blue on the map), no stiles

APPROXIMATE TIME: 2¾ hours

TRAINS: Paddington to Cookham, change at Maidenhead (hourly; from 33 minutes). Elizabeth line, change at Maidenhead (hourly; from Liverpool Street from 59 minutes). Buy a day return to Cookham

MAP: OS Explorer 172 (Chiltern Hills East)

FOOD & DRINK: Lots of places to eat and drink along Cookham High Street

PICNIC: Bench above the escarpment path and then a few along the Thames

TOILETS: Cookham station and junction of High Street and Sutton Road

before a final stretch of riverside walking across marsh belonging to the National Trust. The walk finishes with an amble through Cookham via the churchyard, home to Stanley Spencer's gravestone, past the Stanley Spencer gallery, and up the attractive high street with its many pubs and across Cookham Moor, back to the station.

DIRECTIONS

1. Exit the station and turn left to walk out of the car park onto the road. Turn right along the road. Just before you reach the mini roundabout cross the road.

2. Turn right along the pavement to continue in the same direction and turn left along the drive, in front of the houses.

3. When the track bends to the right continue ahead.

4. At the road turn left and almost immediately right along a car-wide path. Aim for a field gate, go through a gap in the fence to the left of the gate, to join a footpath straight ahead.

5. In 500m ignore a left turn over a railway bridge. Continue ahead through a small section of scrub and then alongside a second section of golf course.

6. Descend wooden stairs and turn left through a large gate and under a railway arch. The path soon forks. Take the right fork and pass through a kissing gate. Continue on this path for just under 500m, until you reach a bench and a board walk over marshy ground on the right.

7. **For the shorter walk**, continue on the footpath at the base of the escarpment until you reach a three-armed footpath signpost with a pool behind. Here pick up the directions from **11** below (but turn right).

8. **For the longer walk**, take the thin footpath on the left, diagonally up the escarpment. The path is steep and can be slippery if wet or frosty.

9. Close to the top of the escarpment follow the path as it bends right and contours round.

10. In 600m you enter woodland, the path soon ends at a car-wide track. Turn right, doubling back on yourself and gradually descend the escarpment.

11. At the bottom you reach a three-armed footpath signpost. Turn left and head towards a field gate. Pass through the kissing gate to the right of the field gate and cross the field.

12. Then follow the footpath sign right to reach the Thames, which you follow for 3km.

13. After about 800m, when you reach a line of houses, go through a gate close to the river to follow the path in front of houses and to reach the Bounty pub.

14. After the pub continue to follow the Thames. The path emerges onto marsh again. Later don't be tempted to follow the line of people veering off across the marsh to a distant car park. Instead, continue along the Thames Path next to the Thames, towards buildings.

15. Pass in front of the CRSC clubhouse and then alongside Bell Rope Meadow. At the end of the 'meadow' turn right to follow the Thames Path sign; you soon walk through the church graveyard and past Stanley Spencer's grave.

16. Continue ahead towards the black and white houses and turn left along the driveway and then right onto the road. Take the first right, Cookham High Street. The station is 1.2km up this road.

17. At the top of the High Street pass the war memorial and walk along the raised tarmac path to the left of the road (across Cookham Moor, owned by the National Trust). When this ends continue on the pavement. Pass a mini roundabout and then cross the road at the zebra crossing (as the pavement ahead soon runs out) and continue in the same direction. You pass the mini roundabout where you turned off originally; the station is straight ahead on the left.

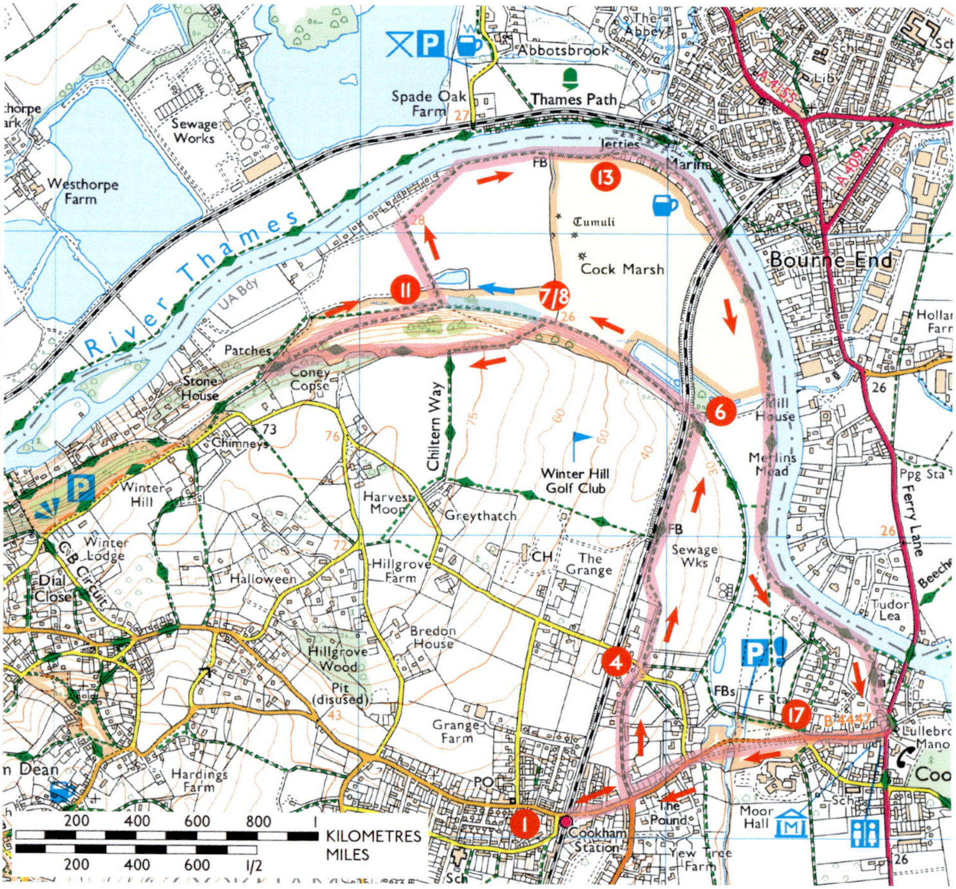

Walk 24

HARLINGTON CIRCULAR, BEDFORDSHIRE

A dramatic snow walk over high Chiltern downland with long views across wintry farmland.

INFORMATION

BEST TIME: When it snows or is frosty
LENGTH & DIFFICULTY: 8 miles (13km); shorter option 5½ miles (9km); several climbs up the Chilterns; the shorter option has a less steep descent. Both moderate
APPROXIMATE TIME: Main walk 4 hours. Shorter option 2¾ hours
TRAINS: Thameslink to Harlington (frequent; from St Pancras 44 minutes). Buy a day return to Harlington
MAP: OS Explorer 193 (Luton)
FOOD & DRINK: The Carpenters Arms in Harlington (closed Mondays)
PICNIC: One bench as you descend on the shorter walk and two on the main walk, on the way to Sharpenhoe Clappers
TOILETS: Harlington station

This circular walk traverses the most easterly block of the Chilterns Area of Outstanding Natural Beauty, which sits north of Luton. More precisely the route runs along the top of the Sundon Hills and the National Trust Moleskin and Markham Hills. It's an easy walk along rounded downland backs, bitten into by wooded combes with a few sheep to keep you company on this little-known part of the Chilterns. The downside is the lack of any pub or cafe along the way, although there is a decent pub at the end in Harlington.

When the snow has disappeared from London streets, it can still be found on the slopes of these north-facing hills and Harlington is on the line to Luton Airport, so trains should keep running in all weathers. Frequent trains prevent a long wait on the return journey: two an hour at the weekend and five an hour on weekday afternoons.

The two-mile hike across farmland to the hills is a pleasure. The fields are stippled with brown clods and stubble and the snow sparkles as you crunch along, as though glitter has been broadcast ahead of you. The neat trails of footprints in the snow, of rabbits, foxes, dogs and birds are almost blue.

Fieldfares, those winter thrushes from Scandinavia and Russia, are flushed from trees and bushes one by one, only to resettle a little further along the hedgerow.

The longer walk reaches Sharpenhoe Clappers, a steep-sided, finger-shaped promontory crowned with a mature beechwood. It is a grand and starkly beautiful place – very atmospheric. The best photographs of the snowy landscape are probably taken from here. The view through the trees looking down to the village and fields below reminds me of Bruegel's Hunters in the Snow. However, for the more

cautious, the steep descent in snow may feel too treacherous. The shorter walk still includes the beauty of a winter beechwood, but has a more gentle descent. The return route follows the bottom of the escarpment, giving you a good view of the hills you walked on earlier. Later a roadside grass verge is wide enough to walk along. Without frozen ground the final mile across fields back to Harlington would be impossibly claggy.

DIRECTIONS

1. Exit the station, turn right and walk to the end of the road. Then turn right over the railway bridge.

2. Just after the bridge, cross over Paxton approach and turn right to walk along its pavement. Continue ahead into an alley.

3. You emerge into a cul-de-sac. After a couple of houses, turn left along a path between houses. Cross the road and continue ahead in the same direction until the road ends. Turn right along what is the main road and after three houses turn right down a footpath that takes you into a new housing estate.

4. Until at least March 2025 (when the footpath reopens) use the alternative route displayed in situ. You return to the main route at point 4a on the map.

5. For the main route, continue on the path parallel to the road for 75m. Shortly after the path bends right, turn left and follow the footpath right then left across fields (which may become housing in the future).

6. In 400m turn right at the footpath sign. Walk along the winding edge of the field for 1.2km. About 250m before the field ends in woodland, turn right uphill on a footpath bordered by trees and shrubbery.

7. In 400m you emerge into a field. Immediately turn left and go through a gap in the hedge onto the downs. Turn right to climb to the top of the hill and then left along the top with the tall hedgerow on your right. In about 400m you come to a road.

8. Turn right along the grass verge and cross the road by a footpath sign and go through a kissing gate. Immediately turn left and go through another kissing gate and follow the wire fence round to the right and make your way up to the top of the downs.

9. Turn left along the top and walk along the undulating downs for about 2km, keeping the hedge (and later just a fence) to your right. At one point the path goes around the head of a wooded combe. Eventually you pass through a kissing gate and walk up steps. Shortly after you enter a wood full of tall beech trees. The path then divides.

10. For the shorter walk take the left path, which leads you slowly downhill; you emerge into a clearing with a bench on your right.

11. Follow the path downhill, through a gate and follow the path diagonally (half-left) across the field, aiming for the left side of a small wood. Exit the field and turn left along the path. (Pick up directions from **23** below.)

12. For the longer walk take the right fork up a small rise. Just after the rise continue ahead at a fairly indistinct footpath crossroads.

13. Eventually you arrive at a few stairs. At the top turn left.

14. In around 300m you arrive at a footpath post where the path divides. Take the right fork. The path soon divides again at field gates. Take the left fork, signposted Chilterns Way.

15. Go through a kissing gate and into a field. The path soon forks, take the right fork aiming for a kissing gate in the far hedge.

16. Cross the road, walk into the car park and continue ahead through two gates on a tarmac path. Shortly before you reach the top of the hill, turn left at a footpath post with a yellow top and enter the woods.

17. In 400m, after you have climbed stairs, you emerge into a meadow. Walk along the top of the meadow into the beech woods.

18. As you enter the woods, the path bends to the right, turn left to climb the mound and make your way to a stone memorial. Drop down to the left to a small path just in front of a low wire fence. Turn right along this path and walk to the end of Sharpenhoe Clappers.

19. At the left end of the promontory, follow the path around to the right and in a few metres turn left down steep steps.

20. At the bottom, as you reach a field, immediately turn left along a footpath. Go through a kissing gate and turn left along the field boundary. In about 100m follow the footpath half-right, crossing the field diagonally, aiming for a kissing gate in the hedge and a house to the left.

21. Cross the road and follow the bridleway ahead for 600m, ignore the first field gate with a National Trust sign. When you come to another field gate, turn right along the bridleway signposted Icknield Way Trail.

22. Follow the path around the field and turn left over a stream. In about 800m you pass a copse and pond on your right (this is where the shorter walk joins).

23. Continue on the track until it ends at a country road. Cross and turn right along the verge.

24. In 400m turn left at a footpath signpost to St Mary's Church 1 mile.

25. Halfway along the field, the path turns into the next field, as directed by a footpath sign. Follow the path across this field. A third of the way along the next field, at a footpath post, bear left into the adjacent field, but continue in the same direction, with a line of trees now on your right.

26. At the next footpath sign, turn right through the hedge and then left to walk uphill to the road.

27. Turn left along the road. Pass a cluster of three houses and turn left along a footpath.

28. When you rejoin the main road turn left. Continue straight ahead at the crossroads to reach the station.

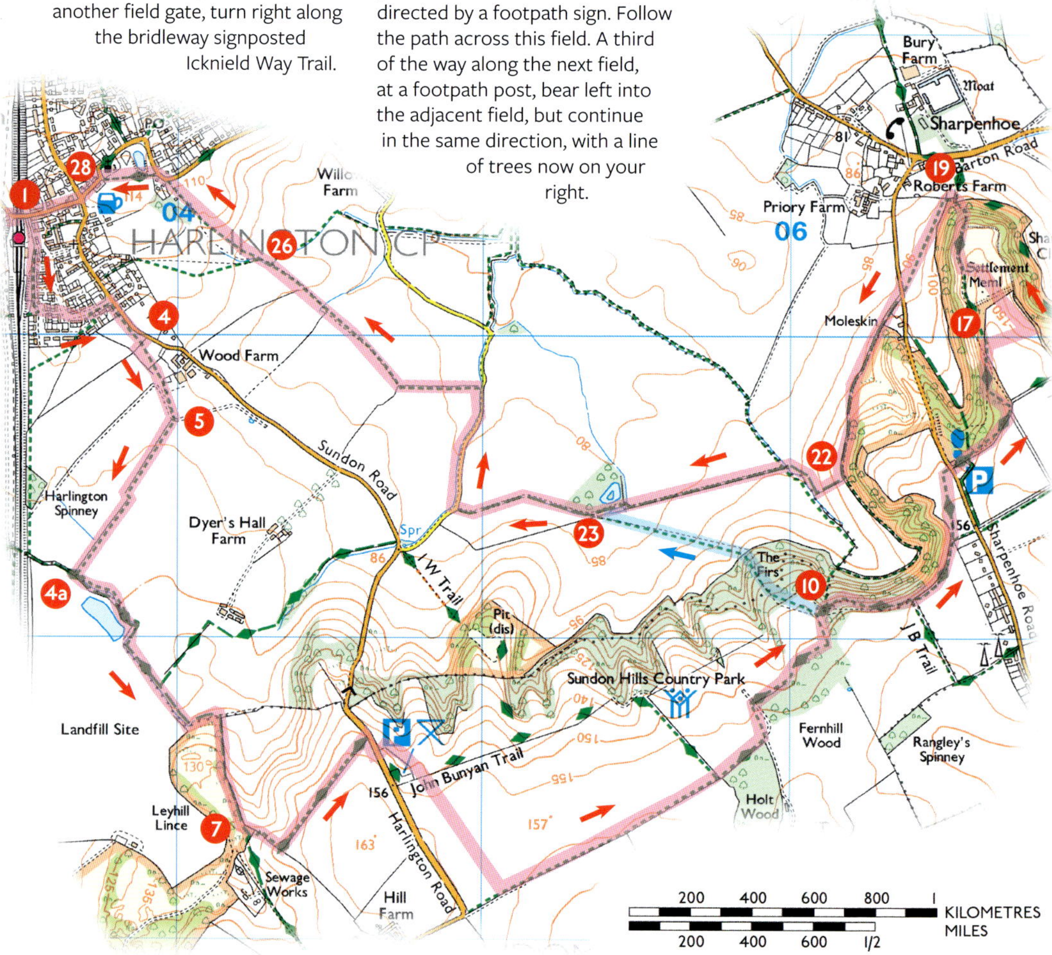

COULSDON CIRCULAR, LONDON

The tamer of the two snow walks and a worthy winter walk in itself.

INFORMATION

BEST TIME: When there's snow or it's frosty
LENGTH & DIFFICULTY: Main walk 6½ miles (10.5km); moderate with a few ups and downs, no stiles. Shorter option 5½miles (9km); easy, with a few ups and downs
APPROXIMATE TIME: Main walk 3¼ hours. Shorter option 2¾ hours
TRAINS: Thameslink to Coulsdon South (twice an hour; from London Bridge approximately 25 minutes) or from Victoria (twice an hour, Sundays hourly; 27 minutes). Coulsdon South is in zone 6 so use contactless or a pass
MAP: OS Explorer 146 (Dorking)
FOOD & DRINK: The Fox, Coulsdon Common
PICNIC: Benches throughout the walk
TOILETS: Coulsdon South station

This one is selected because snow shouldn't prevent you from getting there or back. Coulsdon South station is on the Gatwick Airport line so trains should keep running, and they are regular, so any cancellations or delays shouldn't result in a long wait.

Located in London's green belt and within the M25, this walk explores the largest area of semi-natural downland in Greater London. A highlight of the walk is stumbling across a small Norman church, tucked away down a country lane and home to one of England's most celebrated medieval wall paintings. To warm up, there's a detour to a pub with a fire.

A few minutes after leaving the station you're crunching through snow along the whaleback of Farthing Down. Suburban streets run onto the hills and into the valleys on either side like lava, but peter out as though they've run out of steam. Look back and the tower blocks of Croydon glint in the middle distance and you can just make out the Shard and Docklands' towers on the horizon, sitting under a layer of polluted haze.

As you drop down through a strip of woods to the hidden Happy Valley, you slip away from all urban traces. Snow sweeps down on either side of the dry valley and the fields along the slopes are framed by frosted bushes.

At the end of the long valley it's up through woods again and across fields to the Church of St Peter and St Paul, open in winter between 10am and 3pm. Inside is a quite remarkable Bosch-like cartoon – a doom mural depicting the Last Judgement. Probably painted around 1200 by a travelling monk, the red and yellow ochre painting takes up the whole wall. Its jumble of imps, angels and small characters pitchforked into boiling vats depicts the deadly

sins and issued warnings to the largely illiterate folk of Chaldon.

As you walk back across fields to Happy Valley, black corvids caw in the trees and the sky is full of Gatwick contrails. A shortish detour leads to a pub and then you retrace your steps to Farthing Down and the station.

I've ventured out at 6am, hoping the night's snow in London could still be found in Happy Valley. The station platform at Harringay was wet and dark, with no trace of snow. On the train I craned to see if I could glimpse a dusting along the way, but even as we passed through Croydon I still couldn't spot any. The next stop was Coulsdon South, our destination – and there it was, still hanging on.

As we climbed Farthing Down we walked across snow towards the peachy pink glow of sunrise, with a tiny slither of moon above.

DIRECTIONS

1. From platform 2 don't go over the footbridge – instead turn left down the stairs signposted to Farthing Down. The alleyway will lead you to a road, where you turn left.

2. At the main road turn right and then take the first right, which leads up to Farthing Down. When the road forks, keep to the right. As the road bends right, nip over the road and go through the gate to the right of a cattle grid.

3. Walk along the path to the right of the road, up and along Farthing Down for 1.5km, until you come to a fence that stretches across the width of the down in front of you. Go through the gate.

4. In a few metres turn left along a path and cross the road. Continue straight ahead downhill towards the trees.

5. Continue on the path into the trees, ignoring a path on the right. In a few metres at a footpath crossroads, take the one on the right. The path soon forks at a telegraph pole and bench; take the left fork and this will lead you reasonably gently down to the bottom of Happy Valley.

6. At the bottom, turn right along the base of the valley and follow the path for 1.5km, first between trees (when the path forks take the right fork, keeping to the valley bottom) and then through a more open landscape. Continue along the valley bottom until the valley ends at a wood.

7. At the four-armed footpath signpost, turn right towards Leazes Ave. Follow this footpath for 700m, first uphill through woods and then along a car-wide track with houses on the left.

8. At a three-armed footpath post on the left and a red dog waste bin on the right, turn right along a footpath that eventually ends at a road.

9. Turn right along the road and then almost immediately left to visit the church. When you exit the churchyard, turn left downhill and turn left onto the road joining from the right.

10. In about 50m, turn right through a gap in the hedge onto a footpath signposted Happy Valley ½ mile. Continue on this path up and over the hill. In 700m you pass through a line of trees to reach Happy Valley again. (Follow **11** and **12 for the short route,** which omits the detour to the pub. For the pub go to **13**.)

11. Turn left after the line of trees, passing a footpath signpost and bench on your left, keeping to the top of the field. You'll stay at the same level until you return to Farthing Down.

12. At the end of the field follow the path into woodland and then out again along the top of the next field. At the end of this field rejoin the main walk at **17**.

13. **For the main walk** and the pub go straight down into Happy Valley and up steps on the other side. The pub is about 500m away.

14. At the top turn right along the footpath. The path soon has a thin strip of wood on the left and common on the right. Pass a car park and yellow vehicle gate. The pub is hidden a bit further along on your right.

15. When you leave the pub retrace your steps to the top of Happy Valley. Turn left along the road, which then becomes a footpath.

16. When you arrive back at Happy Valley, follow the path ahead, which is a gentle diagonal descent to the valley floor, past a number of benches. At the valley bottom follow the diagonal path up the other side.

17. Enter the woods in the corner of the field, with a signpost to Farthing Down. When you reach a T-junction turn right.

18. Follow the woodland path until you emerge (600m later) onto Farthing Down. Walk uphill, cross the road and go into the car park.

19. Turn right along the path, just beyond the City of London board, which runs along the spine of the downs until it ends in 1.8km.

20. At the end of the downs retrace your steps to the station. Go through the gate next to the cattle grid. Cross the road to walk downhill on the pavement and turn left onto the main road.

21. Then it's first left and just after the road on the left, turn right down a footpath signposted to the station.

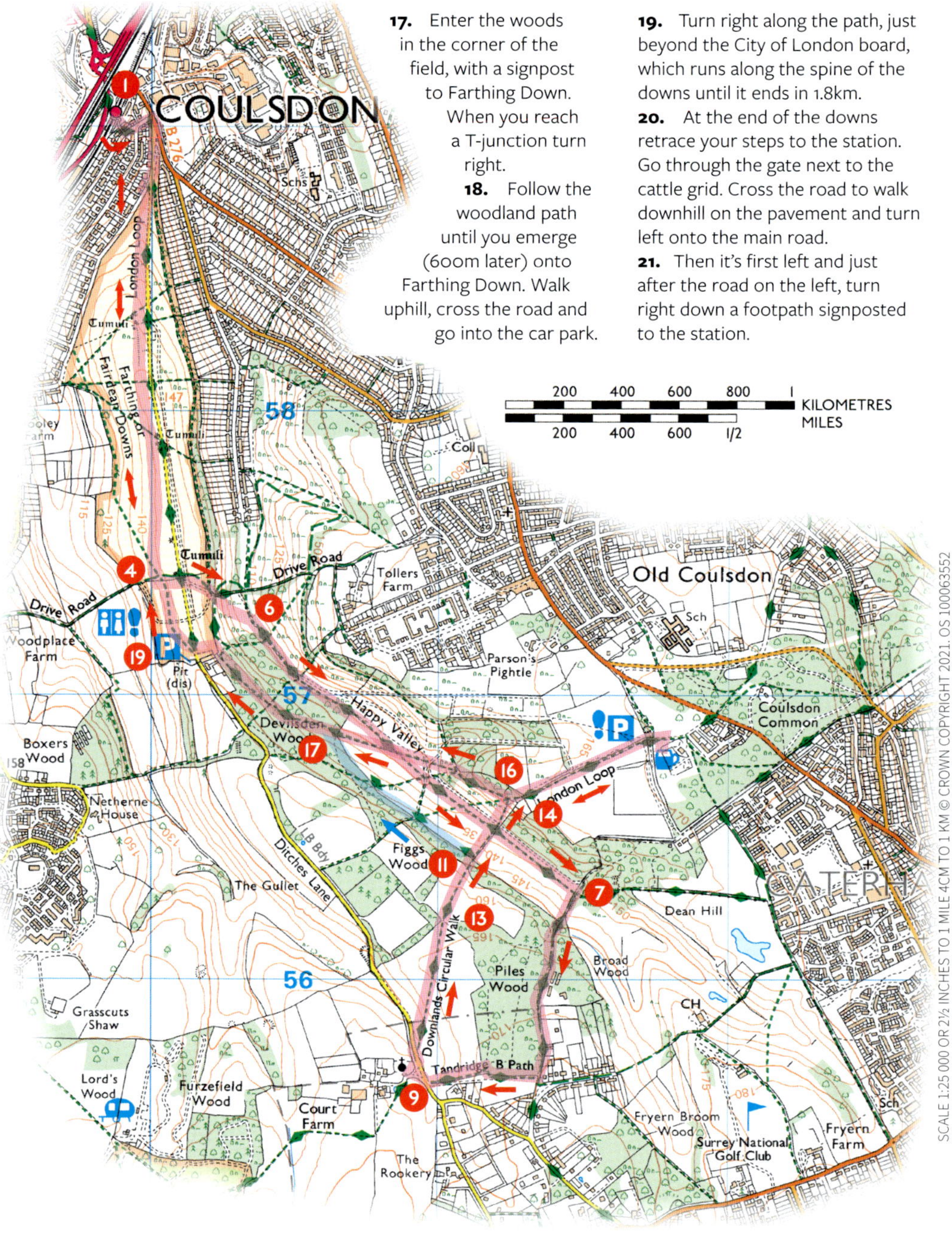

BOX HILL CIRCULAR, SURREY

If you welcome a slightly challenging ramble in winter, you'll enjoy this strenuous walk.

There are steep climbs and sharp descents on this route through the wooded North Downs; at the end, fabulous views stretch out from Box Hill across the Weald to the South Downs 26 miles away.

This is a rewarding walk at any time of the year, but in winter the views are less impeded by trees. Due to its length, the walk fits more comfortably into February's longer days, the same month that catkins quiver on hazel. While the mud shouldn't be too bad, there are muddy sections, so you'll need wellies or walking boots (preferably walking boots to give you a good grip on the slopes).

You start off across water meadows that lead into woodland. After this easy start you hike uphill, perhaps pausing for a drink at the King William IV. The creep of green moss is more noticeable after winter's denuding, rising brightly in small mounds between dead leaves and dressing the base of trees in a furry second skin. At the top of the Mickleham Downs, trunks of silver birch, red lines of dogwood and racemes of yellow catkins add colour to winter's dull background. Here the route runs along the Gallops, a long strip of grassland where Winston Churchill landed his plane when visiting Lord Beaverbrook during World War II. Further on you cross an area of hilly heath before you follow the North Downs Way along the escarpment to Box Hill. On a clear winter's day, the position of the late afternoon sun is just right for taking photos from Box Hill and as you stroll back along a ridge, carpeted in sward, you're bathed in gold light. The mile along pavements back to the station isn't too bad. While you never quite escape the distant rumble of traffic, at the end of this walk I feel I've been truly immersed in countryside.

INFORMATION

BEST TIME: Last week in January and all of February
LENGTH & DIFFICULTY: 9 miles (13km); strenuous with several steep climbs and descents
APPROXIMATE TIME: 4½ hours
TRAINS: Victoria to Box Hill and Westhumble (hourly; 56 minutes) or from Waterloo (hourly; 50 minutes). Buy a day return to Box Hill and Westhumble
MAP: OS Explorer 146 (Dorking)
FOOD & DRINK: King William IV pub (early on and closed Monday and Tuesday) or Stepping Stones pub near the end of the walk in Westhumble
PICNIC: Benches on the Gallops and Headley Heath
TOILETS: None

DIRECTIONS

1. Exit the station and walk up the concrete steps on the left, (not the stairs to the footbridge over the railway line).

2. At the road turn left and walk over the brick railway bridge. Cross the road and follow the footpath straight ahead, with the railway below on your right.

3. When you emerge into the field, keep to the left side. At the end of the field, go through a gate into woods.

4. Keep on the main path for 2km until you emerge from the woods onto a wide tarmac track - ignoring a right fork in 300m (keep the field to the right), later a path on the left, another right fork downhill in 1.4km and other turnings on the way.

5. When you come out of the woods, turn right downhill along the tarmac track. You shortly join a lane, continue downhill. When the lane bends sharply left, continue straight ahead on the footpath (between hedges) downhill.

6. At the bottom, turn right along the tarmac path over the river. At the main road turn left along the pavement. When you reach the bus stop, cross to the central reservation. Turn left along the central reservation until you're opposite the bus stop on the far side and cross the road.

7. Turn right along the pavement and turn left up Byttom Hill. Continue ahead and turn right up steps at the footpath signpost to the King William IV pub. From now on, the route becomes the same as the **National Trust's Box Hill Hike** until you reach Box Hill towards the end of the walk. This route is clearly signposted, so you can put away the instructions until point **27** below. However, if you prefer to read instructions:

8. If you've ventured into the pub, as you go out turn right and up the steps. Continue up this footpath until you reach a footpath crossroads; continue going up along the footpath straight ahead.

9. Towards the top of the hill the terrain flattens out and soon the path forks. Take the right fork.

10. At a footpath crossroads, continue ahead, aiming for a clearing. When you reach the clearing you pass a concrete trig point on your left.

11. A path joins from the right, then the path forks again; take the left fork. Then it forks again; take the right fork and keep going until you see the gallops – a long stretch of grass, like an airstrip.

12. Walk along to the end of the gallops. Go into the woods and past an information board on the archaeology of Mickleham Downs.

13. Shortly after, the path forks; turn right downhill (the descent eventually becomes very steep). The path ends at a road.

14. Cross the road and pick up a footpath to the left of the house. Climb uphill and eventually you come to High Ashurst Outdoor Centre on your right.

15. Just before you reach the driveway go through a gate on the left and walk downhill.

16. When you reach a T-junction turn left along a car-wide track.

17. At the foot of the hill continue ahead to circle the bottom of Headley Heath and then turn right up a flight of steps to reach the ridge (there are some nice picnic benches here).

18. At the top, continue on the main path for 500m until you come to a six-way footpath junction; here you turn right along a wide track.

19. Continue ahead for 250m; the path is initially flat and then goes downhill. You pass through one footpath crossroads and then another further down the hill.

20. Then, still on the same path, go uphill. At the top the path forks; take the left fork. This will eventually bring you to a large information board with a small roof on your right; go through the gate and turn left along the road.

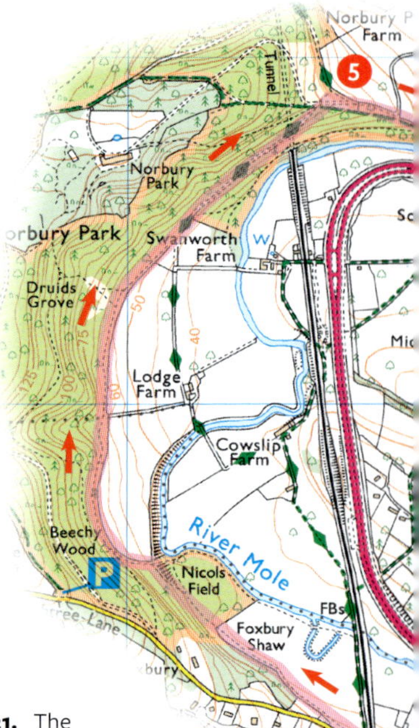

21. The road soon forks. Take the right fork and continue to the end of this road, first with houses on the left and then both sides.

22. When you come to a road, cross the road to continue ahead on a footpath.

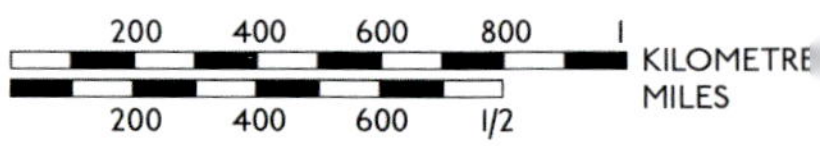

23. The North Downs Way will later join from the left. Continue ahead along the escarpment.

24. About halfway down the hill, turn right up steps to follow the North Downs Way.

25. At the top of the steps, take the footpath that forks to the left. In just over 1km you reach a gate into a garden. Turn left to follow the footpath downhill.

26. At the bottom turn left along the drive. In a few metres turn sharp right at the T-junction up a car-wide track. In 150m the path forks; take the left fork.

27. Go through a kissing gate and take the right fork. You now leave the Box Hill Hike. Turn right to climb up the steep hill, with the fence on your right, to reach the viewpoint.

28. Walk in front of Box Hill viewpoint and continue along the escarpment on a wide path.

29. Continue on this path for 1km, going in and out of woodland, through gates, ignoring several turnings-off to the right and left and keep pretty much to the same level, although rising towards the end. You'll pass the eccentric resident's gravestone on the way.

30. Eventually the path becomes a white chalk path along a thin ridge. Continue ahead down a wide grass slope. As you near the bottom, aim for a wooden fence.

31. Go through the gate in the fence. Cross the road and turn left along the pavement until you're opposite the Burford Bridge Hotel.

32. Cross the road and turn right along the pavement. Keep on the pavement as it bears left past the roundabout and alongside the A road. Keep to the left side and follow the path as it dips and turn right into the subway.

33. At the end of the subway turn left. Then turn right into Westhumble Street, which in 500m will bring you to the station.

Publisher:
Corncockle Publishing
London N8 OBL

Editor: Victoria George

Illustrator: Jennifer Gloster-Kok
jennifergllosterkok.uk

Cover design: Neil Gower

Photographs: Julia Smith

Picture editor: Peter Al-Sheikhli
www.design2d.co.uk

Proofreading: Norma Daykin, Aggie MacKenzie, Maddy Paxman, Laura Smith & Ruth Smith

Design consultant:
Lucy Harper
www.lucyalexandraharper.co.uk

Printed and bound:
In Great Britain by Gomer Press

A catalogue record for this book is available from the British Library
ISBN: 978-1-7399867-1-1

ACKNOWLEDGEMENTS

My favourite way of seeing friends is to go on a walk together. A day out allows us to have long chats while we enjoy the rhythm of walking and the beauty of the countryside. So a big thank you to my walking companions for being up for it, for testing directions and for your wonderful company and friendship: Gillian Arthur, Ross Adams, Patsy Blades, George Clarke, Norma Daykin, Victoria George and Stephen Clark, Janey Hagger, Ellie King Cole and Moira King, Jenny Gloster, Ingrid Kuratle, Maddy Paxman, Laurence Pinterault and Marc Tuft, Sally and Jim Staveley, the rest of the Millers, the Tavi Walking Group (Lis Jones, Pat Key, Louise Lyon and Simon Young), my CDS colleagues, the Norfolk crew and the very special Family Smith: Alfie, Brian, Laura, Paul, Paula, Peter and Ruth.

I am forever grateful to Victoria George, my trusty, eagle-eyed editor and dear friend who has enthusiastically embraced this project from its inception and has supported me so magnificently.

Norma Daykin, Aggie MacKenzie, Laura Smith and Ruth Smith dedicated many hours to the book, proofreading and offering suggestions. Maddy Paxman proof read the second edition. Lucy Harper gave me invaluable help with the design and Peter Al-Sheikhli has done a remarkable job as picture editor, while simultaneously fixing any dusty, badly exposed or wonky photos. The talented Jennifer Gloster has superbly illustrated the book with her exquisite drawings and I was delighted when Neil Gower, internationally acclaimed graphic artist, agreed to produce the cover, which has combined words and image so adeptly. You have all been a delight to work with and so generous with your time and expertise. I couldn't have produced this book without you all – you have helped make it the best it could be.

I must also thank Gareth Acreman at Gomer Press for advice on printing, Nick from Latitude

Maps for providing the Ordnance Survey extracts, and mention Peter Forbes who runs the excellent Narrative Non-Fiction course at City University as well as my fellow students who gave me the confidence and tools to try my hand at writing.

Thanks also to the inspirational curators of walks who have helped me on this quest – in particular the authors of *Time Out Country Walks*, the associated online Saturday Walkers Club and the Pathfinder Guides. I would also like to pay homage to the architects of London's Green Belt, to those who fight to retain our unique web of public footpaths and to all environmental activists.

Finally, and most importantly, to the three main men in my life: Paul my husband and our children Callum and Euan, who have enthusiastically ventured out walking with me and been endlessly supportive and patient as I disappeared for days to work on 'the book'. Thank you for your love, your companionship and for making me laugh. I know how lucky I am to have you.

THE SECOND EDITION

Five years after I'd finalised directions for the first edition, more had changed than I'd anticipated. Housing estates had sprung up, a path had been closed on the Guildford circular, a road fell away revealing the impassable chasm of HS2 on the Wendover route, damage caused by too much footfall in part of the Ashridge Estate became evident, large water-filled cavities close to the surface were discovered at Otford and a section of the coastal path into Hastings was reopened. Consequently, each of these walks has been slightly rerouted.

As anticipated, there were many small changes; stiles had replaced gates, gates had been removed or replaced with kissing gates, metal gates had replaced wooden ones, signposts had disappeared, information boards had been moved, fences had been erected creating 'new' fields and enclosing footpaths. Directions have been tweaked accordingly.

Latest updates can now be found on my website. We're reliant on you alerting other walkers to changes, so please do add your updates here via comments

https://walks4eachseason.blogspot.com
or message me on instagram @jsmithwalks. Thank you.

A couple of years ago, I finally subscribed to the OS Maps Premium app. I wish I'd done so earlier, as it shows you exactly where you are on Ordnance Survey maps. I can't recommend it enough. It's a great companion to this book.

Walks for Each Season was born out of my frustration with going on the same old walks, a desire to explore the range of countryside within reach of London and to make sure no season passed without being out in it, experiencing the best of it, immersing myself in it. The book I needed wasn't available – producing this one was a way to share my discoveries.

I really enjoyed revisiting each walk to check directions for this second edition. I was struck again by what great walks they are. I hope you enjoy them as much as I have.

Julia Smith January 2025